CHURCH WITH NO WALLS - A 21 DAY CHALLENGE

Published in Nashville, Tennessee by Artist Garden Entertainment

Edited by Lindsay Williams

Cover Design and Interior Design by Sarah Siegand

CHURCH
— WITH —
NO WALLS
A 21-DAY CHALLENGE

NOAH CLEVELAND

NASHVILLE, TN

TABLE OF CONTENTS

FOREWORD
BY TONY NOLAN

Before we dive into this book, let me take a moment and tell you about the author. He's got a hero's name, Noah. I can't say that he looks like the guy in the Bible, but I can tell you that he has just as much passion! His heart beats for the glory of God. His lungs expand and contract for the advancement of the Kingdom of God on earth. I like being around those kinds of people, and I love reading their books. You are going to love this book. Why? Because, I'm betting that what happens to me when I hang around Noah is going to happen to you through this book. Your heart is going to beat fervently for God's glory, and you're going to breathe in the wonder of how beautiful the world can be when the Kingdom of God breaks out beyond the walls of the Church.

Now, before you accuse me of overselling this book, pause a moment, and let me tell you why I'm so sure this book will change your life. The first reason is because Noah Cleveland is the real deal. So every principle he presents in the pages ahead isn't theory, it's firsthand practice from a man who has faithfully and fervently served the Lord for years. He grinds it out in beat-up hotel rooms, bumper-to-bumper traffic, hard labor load-ins and loud-outs, and countless late-night hours counseling and ministering to hearts that have been crushed by the fallout of a sin-cursed world. He's #legit! However, I still don't think I've successfully communicated just how exceptional Noah is and how intent he is about being a man who lives out the mantra of a Church with no walls. So, I'm going to tell you a little story...

The darkest, scariest storm clouds that I've ever seen rolled in, and I thought, I'm not going to be able to preach, and we are all going to die! It was only minutes before I was to take the stage at an outdoor festival in Alabama. As I mused at the madness hovering before me, an elderly man blurted out, "Naw, it ain't goin' to rain!" His wrinkled face and wind whipped hair, coupled with his deep, crackly voice, made me think I was looking at Johnny Cash. Standing side stage, his eyes were wide, staring at the apocalyptic storm front. His mouth was twice as wide as his eyes, and his hands were clasped together at his chest in a prayer position. I think he was saying a prayer more than he was making a statement. I was just about to tell him that he had great faith, when a G5 wind gust nearly knocked me over at the same moment a nuclear-infused lightening bolt cut through the sky. There was no time to count seconds to see how far the lighting struck from us. The explosion of thunder shook our clothes, and now my eyes and mouth were wider than his, and my hands joined his in the prayer position! I thought, This guy has the worst prayer life I've ever seen, and I just might be a prophet, because we're definitely going to die!

Then came the rain! It fell hard, fast, and furious! It succeeded in what the wind and lighting couldn't do. I hit the ground. I've never seen it rain that hard. Do you remember the viral "Ice Bucket Challenge" videos? I saw one where a guy filled up a John Deere Front Loader and had the water dumped on him. I guess he was trying to be creative, but he almost got killed by the massive weight of the water dropping all at once. That's what happened to us on that open field! People were falling everywhere, and those who somehow managed to stay up, darted for cover. I got up and raced to my car. As I sat there listening to myself pant, the roar of rain crashed down on the hood of my car, and I thought, This is over, and I might as well head back to the hotel room. The thrashing trees, bending almost to the point of snapping, told me I was thinking correctly. As I put the car in drive, I noticed the face of my cell phone light up in the darkness. Noah Cleveland was calling. I swiped right and heard, "Tony, I'm going to the pavilion! People are seeking shelter under it. Come join me. I'll see ya there." Then I lost the signal or Noah hung up; I'm not sure. I sat there thinking, This guy really thinks he is Noah! The flood is raging. We need to seek higher ground, and Noah wants to gather 2 x 2 x 200 or any number for that matter, under a pavilion? He is crazy! Or maybe he is #legit?

I chided myself for not replacing my windshield wipers I had promised I would get next time I went to Wal-Mart as I tried to drive, inch by inch, with the ability to only make out what was before me for a fraction of a second between the swish of the blades. To beat it all, my eyeglasses started fogging up, too.

I still don't know how I made it to that pavilion. Once I arrived, I sprinted from the car to the massive crowd of people who had gathered. There were no walls, just a roof and a few old picnic tables underneath. Noah was standing on one of the tables! I used my finger to clear the lens on my glasses, and my eyes focused in on Noah, head back, mouth open, voice bellowing, and arms strumming an acoustic guitar. A storm did not stop the Noah of the Bible from worshipping God, nor was this one going to stop Noah Cleveland. No amplifiers, no lights, no fog machine, just a powerful voice and a passionate heart. He took us to the throne of God! Every cold, rain-soaked human being under that covering felt the warmth of a heart ablaze for the glory of God. He led them to sing, and they did! What lighting? What thunder? What rain? Maybe ole "Johnny Cash" was right. Not that it wouldn't rain, but that it would not, and could not, stop the man of God from His Kingdom mission.

Noah gave me a wink and a nod to jump up on that table with him. And I did. He just has that kind of effect on people. Like I said, that's why you are going to be changed through this book.

That rainy day, Noah strummed a final chord, and when the voices from the crowd faded, I belted out the Gospel. Social media posts later revealed some amazing pictures of that moment. Noah, leading us to the God who forgives and empowers us to new life; and me, no mic, massive crowd, with my hands cusped around my mouth inviting people to embrace Jesus and life in His Kingdom. It's a Kingdom without walls, a city up on a hill, unable to be hidden, shining for every soul lost in the darkness to come to its rescuing power. Many did that day, and many more will, after absorbing this book.

I wish I could tell you that, in life, it's not going to rain. But I can't, because the clouds are gathering even as you read this. We all suffer from the storms of life. People in your neighborhood, at your school, and at your work place, stand eyes wide, mouth open, gazing at news headlines and Instagram posts that take our breath and knock us down emotionally. The events surrounding 9/11, beheadings, riots, suicide bombings, and people in the streets of New York getting run down by a car while they innocently tour the city, serve as a barometer of sorts. It's going to rain. But God has a covering, and it has no walls. It's His Church. It is made of people of all walks of life who help one another walk through life. It's going to rain, but be of good cheer, Jesus has overcome the rain, through His Church with no walls.

—Tony Nolan, fellow member of the Church with no walls

INTRODUCTION

Albert Einstein once said, "Nothing happens until something moves." That seems like an understatement, and one that's blatantly obvious. Everywhere you look in the world today, you'll see proof that this statement is true, and it's even truer in the Church. The lack of moving on behalf of God's people is disturbing and should be cause for alarm. It's easy to sit around and point fingers, but being part of the solution is another story. When the rubber meets the road, where is our action? Where is our faith when it's time to move?

This book is meant to encourage you to move, and to move a lot. You are about to go on a journey filled with action. You'll encounter many people and problems in need of a solution, but the solution starts with you. For the next twenty-one days, my prayer will be that you'll operate beyond your comfort zone and outside the walls of a church building. However, I know this is easier said than done. When our comfort zone is challenged, it's easy to turn back to what is most familiar. I have personally found that one of the hardest obstacles to overcome when doing ministry "outside the walls" is breaking the ice. This is especially the case when I'm engaging with someone I don't know. Do you have that same problem? How do we initiate the conversation? What words or angles do we use to get the ball rolling? For me, once the ice is broken, things become much easier. What if I told you God has already broken the ice for you? Have you ever thought about the fact that the Holy Spirit has gone before you and is preparing the way? Could it be when God speaks to you to serve, love, give, share, or just talk to someone that He's setting the whole thing up? Someone's heart could be in perfect shape to be touched by God, and you get to be a part of that.

There's a story in Acts 8 about a man named Philip that paints this picture perfectly:

"Now an angel of the Lord said to Philip, 'Rise and go toward the south to the road that goes down from Jerusalem to Gaza.' This is a desert place. And he rose and went. And there was an Ethiopian, a eunuch, a court official of Candace, queen of the Ethiopians, who was in charge of all her treasure. He had come to Jerusalem to worship and was returning, seated in his chariot, and he was reading the prophet Isaiah. And the Spirit said to Philip, 'Go over and join this chariot.' So Philip ran to him and heard him reading Isaiah the prophet and asked, 'Do you understand what you are reading?' And he said, 'How can I, unless someone guides me?' And he invited Philip to come up and sit with him." (Acts 8:26-31, ESV)

In this scripture, we see that the Holy Spirit had already broken the ice for Philip. The Ethiopian was already curious and reading the Bible, but yet he didn't understand it. God then speaks to Philip a simple word: "GO!" He told him to go over to the chariot. Philip had no idea who the man was or what he was doing, but when he got there, the ice was already broken. He was able to share Jesus with him and later baptize him. It was a divine appointment set up by the Holy Spirit working in both of them at the same time, and a miracle happened. Philip not only went, he went quickly. Verse 30 tells us "he ran to him."

God is wanting to use you just like He used Philip. There are people all around us every day that God wants us to run to. We need to have that same urgency Philip had when the Holy Spirit commissions us to act.

One of my good friends in ministry once told me, "The Church doesn't exist for us. The Church exists for the world." How many times have we made the Church look the way we want it to look? How many times have our desires kept us inside the building rather than going outside to reach the world around us? How many times have we made Church about us?

The team Jesus assembled did most of their ministry outside the walls of a church building. They never had a worship team to help set the atmosphere, nor did they have to be on a stage to love people. They didn't need to preach behind a pulpit to open the Bible and share the Gospel. As a matter of fact, we only have one recorded sermon from Jesus, The Sermon on the Mount. The rest of His ministry was done while serving others outside the walls of the Church. There were no walls that kept Him in or kept others out. He just simply walked through life loving and serving people. If we are to be a follower of Christ, we need to walk as Jesus walked. The very definition of a Christian is to be Christ-like. As Christians, we are called to emulate and resemble Jesus every day whether we're with family, with friends, at school, at work, at home, or anywhere in between. Jesus followers constantly break down walls of pride, fear, anxiety, rejection, failure, insignificance, denomination, culture, race, and any other obstacle keeping them confined inside the walls. With persistence, the walls will fall. I have found that sharing the love of Jesus is like most things; it's challenging at first, but it becomes easier and more familiar to us the more we do it.

Being authentic is important as we operate outside a building. It's easy to look at a public figure, like a pastor, and think we have to say and do exactly what they do; but the truth is, God wants to use our personality. He desires to use our stories, talents, abilities, and uniqueness. You possess gifts and abilities that I don't have, which is why we make up the body of Christ. Being a part of the body of Christ makes you valuable to the Kingdom. We invest time to learn how to do so many other things that are really hard to accomplish in life, so what if we took a similar approach in learning how to share the Gospel with people? For me, it was difficult at first, but it quickly became part of my life and existence as a believer. When we make serving others a priority, our DNA changes, and we start to resemble Jesus.

So for the next twenty-one days, I am challenging you to break down the walls in your life. In doing so, you'll begin to look more and more like the disciples Jesus sent out into the world. Matthew 5:14 says, "You are the light of the world. A city on a hill cannot be hidden." It's time for your faith to turn into action.

As you read through this book, each chapter will consist of a daily devotion, a word of encouragement from people who make up the Church from all walks of life, and a challenge or set of challenges that will ask you to step out of your comfort zone and engage the world around you. The challenges are there to help encourage you to take your faith outside the four walls of a building. I chose to write this book in a daily challenge/devotional format because I believe a call to action is something we all can benefit from and need from time to time. I have found in my own life there are seasons where I get complacent and too comfortable with my faith, and it results in a very stale and stagnant approach to sharing the Gospel with others. The challenges in this book are also meant to stretch and help you see new and creative ways that God may want to use you for His Kingdom.

The section called "A word from the Church" is written by the Church. A Church with no walls isn't made up of one person, so I thought it was fitting to find people who have great insight on the topics ahead.

You can make this book part of your quiet time each day, part of your daily devotional, or the start of something totally new in your life. Some of these challenges will be easier than others, but I ask that you make it a priority to carry all of them out every day no matter how it looks or when it takes place. Take each challenge presented in the pages ahead seriously. Be consistent with your approach. Take notes about your experiences in a journal after each challenge or day is complete.

I believe when you cross the finish line, you will be amazed to look back at what you wrote down along your journey. Listen to that still small voice inside you and go forth with courage and boldness. I believe if you take this challenge, you will see a significant change in your approach to being a follower of Christ. I know I have. It's time for us to start tapping into our calling and who we're really meant to be, and that's a Church with no walls.

"Faith apart from works is dead."
(James 2:26, ESV)

CHURCH WITH NO WALLS

Written By Noah Cleveland, Nathan Nockels, Tony Wood

Stones we were stacking

Are on the ground

They stood between us

We tore them down

Nothing but love in their place

We are the body, His hands and feet

Brothers and sisters, One family

Let nothing separate, Are you with me

Let this world hear us say

We are the church

The church with no walls

Shout to this city

Come one come all

Let division disappear

Everybody's welcome here

We are the church with no walls

Bring all your failures

Bring all your shame

We are the fallen

Who found God's grace

There is nothing to fear love is waiting

Mercy and hope are right here

So we sing with one voice
All together shout with joy
This is our anthem
This is a holy roar

We are the church
The church with no walls
Shout to this city
Come one come all
Let division disappear
Everybody's welcome here
We are the church with no walls

LISTEN ON:

DAY 1:

SCRIPTURE

*"In the beginning was the Word,
and the Word was with God,
and the Word was God."*

John 1:1 (ESV)

"

IT AIN'T THE PARTS OF THE BIBLE THAT I CAN'T UNDERSTAND THAT BOTHER ME, IT'S THE PARTS THAT I DO UNDERSTAND.

— MARK TWAIN

DAY 1:

SCRIPTURE

The best thing in my life of thirty-one years, outside of my salvation, was meeting my beautiful, smart, kind, anointed, gifted, and smoking hot wife, Ivy! We were high school sweethearts, so we've basically grown up together. She is my soulmate, partner in ministry, and the one who knows me best. It's such an awesome blessing to have a wife who is godly and a best friend I can constantly share every thought and experience with.

Walking through this journey of life together has taught me many things about her. I know where we went on our first date, where we had our first kiss, what her favorite color is, her favorite foods, favorite movies, favorite vacation spot, and, of course, I know our wedding anniversary (June 7 #browniepoints). I also know what she's going to say about a sink full of dishes, the grass growing too high, the trash stinking up the house, and if I work too many hours. I know these things and many more because of all the times she's left me very "nice" letters that tell me what needs to be done. She makes sure the directions are loud and clear through her words. There's not much arguing when it's written down. And if I read it differently than how she intended it, a mess occurs— mostly for me. And let me tell you, there are many days I need a list to look at, or it will simply "slip my mind," or so she thinks!

Much like my wife's "reminder notes," one of the greatest benefits we have of being followers of Christ is His letter to us. The Bible is God's Word directly from His mouth to His children. "The Lord said" is written over three thousand times in the Bible, followed by quotes directly from God. The Bible is a book written over a fifteen hundred year span, over forty generations, by more than forty authors from every walk of life, on three continents, and in three languages; but yet, it is perfectly woven together with no discrepancies. No book has sold more copies than the Bible. That sounds like a book I need to read.

The Bible gives us direction and serves as an anchor for our lives. Many of you reading this would never argue that, but if you're like me, sometimes just finding time to read it can be a challenge in and of itself. Reading Scripture requires great discipline and consistency. It's kind of like that diet we start at the beginning of each new year, which requires incredible discipline in our eating habits to see real results. We stick to it for a few days, maybe even a few weeks, but once the busyness of life kicks in, our "fat man" mentality takes over again.

> The Bible gives us direction and serves as an anchor for our lives.

Jesus constantly quoted Scripture to everyone He encountered; yet most of us rarely use it in conversation. In my life I've found this to be the result of one thing, and that's simply the lack of reading it. I can never give someone something I don't have. So if God's Word has not been deposited inside of me, then there is nothing for me to draw from when the time comes. One of the worst feelings for me as a minister and artist is to find myself onstage in front of people, only to realize there's nothing to draw from in that season of my life.

God's Word is alive and powerful, and although my words or songs can bring people to tears, or draw other emotions out of them, they are powerless if not backed by Scripture. Reading and knowing God's Word is a key component to becoming a true and effective follower of Jesus. It is a true cornerstone in our personal lives, families, and callings. We are all called to know God and make Him known (Matthew 28:19), and it's impossible to know Him without knowing His Word. It's also impossible to make Him known, if we don't know Him first.

Psalm 119:105 says, "Your Word is a lamp to my feet and a light to my path." We need light to help us do everything. Have you ever tried to read, write, drive, or do almost anything outside in the dark without a light? It's impossible. I love playing golf, but there's a reason the clubhouse shuts down after the sun sets. Scripture truly is the light in a dark place. Understanding Scripture is imperative to becoming a more effective disciple, especially when journeying outside the walls of your local church.

If God's Word really lights our way, then why do we have such a hard time heading in the right direction? I have found myself, on more than one occasion, in the wrong place or heading down the wrong road. The first thing I do is ask God why things are going wrong or look out of place. I think, Maybe God is trying to teach me something. Later I realize the cause of all the strife and heartache was because I wanted to call the shots. I wanted to be the one making the decisions and creating the path. I thought my knowledge and emotions alone were enough to lead me, but I never once allowed the Word of God to light up my path and show me what direction was best. I have learned the hard way, over and over again, that God's Word is the ultimate compass.

5

A WORD FROM THE CHURCH...
By Blake Reynolds, Pastor of One Church in Cadiz, KY

I love Scripture because it works in every area of life for me. Obviously, being a pastor I use it to preach from, but it has much daily use. I've used it to battle the enemy when he's getting in my head. I've used it to pray over my wife and kids. And one of the coolest uses of it is being able to share it with lost people who don't know Jesus.

I remember sitting at a table full of atheists giving me all their reasons why my God wasn't real, but something changed when I started sharing the Gospel with them. What was so powerful was by the end of our conversation, two of them were weeping, and one wanted to give his life to Jesus.

So if we as Christians say we believe in Jesus, we also have to accept that His Word is living, powerful, and sharper than any two-edged sword that will bring down strongholds. His Word is still alive today! Nothing compares to it. It's time to pick up your Bible, read it, then watch what God can do in you and through you!

TODAY'S CHALLENGE

If Scripture plays a key part in lighting up the way in our lives, then I believe it's a great place for us to start on this twenty-one day journey. Each day there will be Scripture for you to read to start you off in your challenge.

1) **Read Matthew 4.** Notice that Jesus, who has yet to start His ministry at the time, uses Scripture to fight off temptation from Satan. After His time of testing was over, He began to preach, build His team, and do miracles.

2) **Share something you learned or received from this Scripture with one person.**

3) **Post a scripture on your social media platform.**

PRAYER

Lord, I ask that You will give me courage and boldness today to share Your Word with whomever You lead me to share it. Let my mind and spirit become aware of the leading of the Holy Spirit as to when and how to share it. I ask that You'll give me the right words to say, and that You'll help me remember the things that I read. Allow them to be personal to me first, so I can share Your truth with conviction and power. In Jesus' name, amen.

DAY 2:
LOVE

"If I speak God's Word with power, revealing all His mysteries and make everything plain as day, but don't have love, I'm nothing."

1 Corinthians 13:2 (MSG)

"

LOVE IS LIFE.
AND IF YOU
MISS LOVE,
YOU MISS LIFE.

— LEO BUSCAGLIA

DAY 2:
LOVE

Jesus replied: "LOVE the Lord Your God with all your heart, and
with all your soul, and with all your mind.
This is the first and greatest commandment.
And the second is like it: love your neighbor as yourself."
Matthew 22:37-39 (NIV)

I remember it like it was yesterday. I was finally getting to go home and take a break from my first year of college. It was almost Christmas, and I was in a hurry to get home to see my mama and get all the benefits that came with being at home like her southern homestyle cookin', staying up all night, sleeping all day, and basically doing whatever I wanted, with no responsibilities.

As I was heading down the highway in my '94 Chevy Blazer, I passed a car that had broken down by the side of the road. Now, I'm sure I had passed many cars up to that point in my driving career of a whopping three years, but this one was different for some reason. I felt something inside me say, "turn around." But wait; what about all those scary movies I'd watched where turning around was a bad idea? I even laughed out loud as I came up with all these different scenarios where I'd be kidnapped by a stranger, and wondered what I was supposed to do. At the time I was eighteen years old and certainly not a mechanic, so my role in this deal was confusing. As I continued to head home, the feeling inside just would not go away, and I couldn't ignore it. I knew I had to turn around and go help this person in whatever way God led me to do so.

As I came back over the crest of the hill and saw the red truck still parked on the shoulder of the road, fear began to overwhelm me. It was not a fear for my safety, but of what my purpose was in this situation. What was I supposed to say or do? I knew God set up this whole scenario, and I was right where I needed to be, but it was still really uncomfortable for me. So I prayed that God would give me boldness and the words to say right before I stepped out of my vehicle to meet this stranded driver.

As I approached this total stranger, the man looked stressed. I introduced myself, and we shook hands. His entire shirt was drenched in sweat as he asked me if I knew how to change a tire. I had a very selfish thought, Yes I do, but don't you know how to, as well? He quickly made me aware of a disability that prevented him from lifting or doing almost anything that put stress on his back, so he was physically not able to change the flat tire. To make matters worse, he didn't even have a jack. He had been trying to change this tire all by himself, with no way to lift the truck up off the ground to even get the tire off. Now I am not that old, but in 2004 cell phones were not in the hands of every person, and this man didn't own one. He had no way of calling for help, so he truly was in desperate need for someone to stop and assist him. I told him I had a tire changing kit in the back of my vehicle, so I went to grab it. As I made my way back to my car, I immediately realized what my purpose in this scenario was, and that was to simply serve him and show him love. There really were no magic words I used that day, only actions of love.

Simply being available for him and showing him kindness was all he needed in that moment.

I figured I'd never see the elderly man again, but that act of love left a huge mark on him. That moment impacted him enough for him to remember my name years later when he was visiting my grandmother's church. He overheard her mention my name one Sunday morning and asked her how she knew me. When she said, "He's my grandson," the man smiled and said, "That young man is the reason I am in church today." He proceeded to tell her how more cars than he could count passed by him that day without stopping, as he sat stranded helplessly, until a young man came to his rescue. It was a divine moment and the very moment that he realized God was real and actually cared about him. Until my Grandmother told me his story, I never knew that minutes before I pulled up, he had prayed and asked God to send Him a sign that He loved him. He was very broken, and little did I know that my simple act of love was the answer to his prayer. As I mentioned in the introduction, God had already broken the ice, and all I needed to be was available to Him!

I've often wondered what would have happened to the man had I not stopped that day. What if I had been in too much of a hurry or too busy with my own selfish desires and just shrugged off the prompting of the Holy Spirit to stop? Thankfully, I followed the nudge from God and experienced what it truly means to be a "church with no walls." I know there have been many other scenarios just like this one where I didn't stop, but this story serves as a reminder to me many days—and I hope it does for you, too—that we should never ignore a whisper from the Holy Spirit.

To follow Jesus means we have to love people not only inside the Church, but also outside the walls. I have to make sure

I am keenly aware when God puts people directly in my path for me to love. I don't always know what to say or what to do when I act on what I'm feeling, but the Lord makes it evident when I step out in faith. The first step is to be obedient to what the Holy Spirit is leading me to do and then follow His direction. Whether it's helping a stranger change a tire, paying for someone's gas when they've lost their wallet, stopping to help someone pick up groceries that dropped out of a torn grocery bag, or letting a stranger skip ahead of you in line because their kids are screaming, we can all find ways to show love to someone. We don't have to preach a sermon in order for them to feel the love of Jesus.

Our flesh is very selfish, and usually it's not going to be the one urging us to do these things. So stay alert because it very well could be the Holy Spirit speaking to you. And just like in my story, you may be exactly who someone needs to encounter today.

A WORD FROM THE CHURCH...
By Jason Lyle, Founder of 10:15 Foundation and Missionary to Uganda, Africa

"If I give away all I have, and if I deliver up my body to be burned, but have not love, I gain nothing." (1 Corinthians 13:3, ESV).

For centuries the Church has tried to contain God inside a building. I remember being a child and hearing the Church referred to as "God's house," as if that's where we went to meet Him. But God cannot be contained by buildings, denominations, or belief systems. God resides in love. Jesus said all moralistic problems are solved in love (Matthew 22:34-37), yet the Church as an organization, at times, puts morality before love. Maybe if we loved first, we could see a true morality come to us, a morality that would be enduring. Take the time today to love someone. You will find it changes you more than it changes them.

TODAY'S CHALLENGE

Most of us think of ourselves as a loving person, but let's take a look at what Jesus said about love, and see if our love matches the love He showed.

1) **Read Mark 12:28-34.** Jesus tells us the greatest commandment is to love. He says something that may be obvious to many of us, which is to love God, but notice how He throws in loving other people in the same sentence. In order to love God, we have to love people. One can't happen without the other.

2) **Find a way to show love to one person.**

PRAYER

God, first of all, teach me how to love You so that I can love others. Jesus was the perfect example of love and compassion, and today I ask You to help me resemble and emulate His love. Help me be aware and listen to the Holy Spirit when He urges me to act in love. I ask you to give me boldness and compassion when the time is right today. In Jesus' name, amen.

DAY 3:
YOUR STORY

"But God chose what is foolish in the world to shame the wise."

1 Corinthians 1:27 (ESV)

"

YOUR STORY IS A KEY THAT CAN UNLOCK SOMEONE ELSE'S PRISON, SO SHARE IT FOR THEIR SAKE.

— UNKNOWN

DAY 3:
YOUR STORY

One of the greatest stories in the Bible, to me, is the story of Peter. I can relate to his story in so many ways. He was just an average guy before he met Jesus. He was also a fisherman, and being a fisherman in that day could have easily meant he was in some way a reject or failure. Most young boys brought up in the Jewish culture of that day would have aspired to be a religious leader of some type, and that started by following a rabbi and becoming one of their disciples.

The fact Peter was a fisherman could have signaled the fact that he was rejected as a disciple. He may have even thought of himself as a man who wasn't cut out to be a leader, so he fell back on his father's craft. Fishermen in that day were considered to be the low men on the totem pole. So early on, when we first meet Peter, we see a young man who is not qualified to be a disciple, let alone a disciple of the Messiah.

After being chosen by Jesus, Peter's world was rocked. He started seeing life through a whole new set of eyes. He was sent out to preach. He watched the Son of God cast out demons, heal the sick, feed five thousand men with just five loaves of bread and two fish, walk on water, and much more. Not only did he see Jesus walk on water, Jesus asked Peter to walk on water as well. Yet, unlike Jesus, he quickly found himself sinking. That's when

God asked Peter to turn his eyes only to Jesus. Just like Peter, if we focus on the chaos and circumstances in our lives, we will sink; but if we turn to Jesus, we will see God at work in a mighty way writing our custom-made story.

There's no telling how many miracles Peter witnessed over the next few years of Jesus' ministry, but even with all the evidence proving He was the long-awaited Messiah, Peter still failed miserably when it seemed to matter most. Jesus told him he would deny Him three times, and that's exactly what happened. Matthew 26:69-74 tells us people exposed him on the night Jesus was arrested. They recognized him easily and even said the way he talked gave him away. Even though he was caught red-handed, Peter walked away in denial. Does that sound familiar?

I don't know about you, but the next few days would have been a low point in my life. The man that I followed and had a front row seat to watch do ministry in a powerful and miraculous way is now dead. Not only is He dead, I failed Him at the most critical time. This part of Peter's story would be a tough thing to bounce back from for anyone. The good news for him, and for us, is Jesus bounced back from death. His victory was our victory. David Crowder says it so well in his song "My Victory": "A cross meant to kill is my victory." What a feeling it must have been to see Jesus alive after watching Him die on a cross just a few days earlier! His story was becoming our story.

Peter's story gets really good in Acts 2. Here's a man who had recently denied Jesus. Now he's marching boldly into the world for the sake of the Gospel, charging hell with a water pistol. What a comeback story! How could an unqualified reject and failure now be used by God to see three thousand people saved in one day? The answer lives inside of all believers...the Holy Spirit. The boldness Peter had in the book of Acts came only from the Holy Spirit and was the key part of his ministry.

I'm sure he never thought in a million years he'd be telling his story of rejection and failure to so many. It takes boldness sometimes for us to share our story, no matter what's written in the pages, but we've all got one to tell. No one can share your story like you can. It was written just for you. Someone once told me, "When it's personal, it's powerful." Sharing your personal story will come with power and conviction because you walked down that path yourself. No one could have told Peter that he didn't walk on water, or deny Jesus, or even see Jesus after He had risen. These were his personal experiences worth sharing with others, and when he told people about them, they listened and believed because he said it with conviction.

Nothing helps someone connect with us better than them saying, "me too." The enemy wants us to feel isolated and alone, but telling our story gives us a huge tool to relate with others.

The enemy tells us lies like, "You're the only one who struggles with this" and "You'll never overcome that." I'm sure you've heard those words, just as I have. He also wants us to feel like the world around us will judge us or look down on us because of our past or what we are going through in the present. All of that is a lie from the very pit of hell, and you are in no way bound by any of it. I have found a continued power and freedom the more

> "I've never walked in your shoes, but I've been on your block."
>
> **- Tony Nolan**
> World Renowned Speaker and Evangelist

I share my story. Some of my story was very difficult to share at first, but now I have seen how it gives hope to others.

Be encouraged today that the world needs to hear your story, as well, and it's time for you to share it. Only God can turn a mess into a message, a test into a testimony, a trial into triumph, and a victim into victory. When you share your story, people will hear and see the evidence of the Almighty God at work in your life. And if He can do it for you, then He can do it for them. That will be a great encouragement to them in their own story. Also remember, the more you share it, the easier it will become.

A WORD FROM THE CHURCH...
By Kevin Hawkins, Store Manager at Home Depot

Growing up in an environment of neglect because of a home ruled by addiction, I adopted many false perceptions of myself and what I was capable of becoming. It was a place that taught me to have limitations and accept failure. Failure became a mindset for me. I never thought I was good enough. This was ingrained in me until a few people told me their story and helped me understand that I was important and had potential.

I came to know Jesus in my car while I was on a drug run. Delivering drugs was my job at the time, until I finally began to understand that I was important simply because I had a God who wanted to know and use me. God radically changed my life and started using my story. He opened up doors to a new career path and gave me a deep passion to reach young people in communities like the one I grew up in. I want them to know they, too, are important and can accomplish any dreams they have. And just like God opened up doors for an unqualified white boy from the hood to be a store manager at one of the most profitable Home Depot stores in the nation, He could do the same for them. I tell my story because I want them to believe in theirs.

TODAY'S CHALLENGE

No one can take away your personal experiences. Many of our storms, heartaches, and victories take place to build our story. Without a valley, there's no mountaintop. We learn the most in life when going through pain. As Christians, we have to have something to say to people, and our personal experiences make that possible. Think about how God has used victories as well as difficult circumstances in your life to draw you closer to Him.

1) **Read Acts 3.**

2) **Write your story down on paper.**

3) **Share your story with someone today.** This may be your first time ever sharing your story, so rehearse it if needed. You may even want to consider making a quick video or written testimony to share on social media.

PRAYER

God, I come before you right now and thank you for what You've done in my life. I thank You for salvation and the victory I have in Jesus. I know You want to use my story to minister to someone else, and I ask You to help me share it today. Lead me to the right person (or people) with whom to share it. In Jesus' name, amen.

DAY 4:

YOUR PLATFORM

"They said to one another, here comes that dreamer."

Genesis 37:19 (ESV)

"

IMAGINE THE POSSIBILITIES WHEN ONE FOCUSES ON THE PLATFORM GOD GIVES THEM INSTEAD OF THE PLATFORM HE GIVES SOMEONE ELSE.

— KEITH STANCIL

YOUR PLATFORM

We can all name celebrities who have huge platforms. We follow many of them on social media. Some use their platforms to raise awareness for political purposes, endorse certain companies, or bring attention to racial issues, sickness or disease. Others use their platform for religious purposes, but also, for their own advancement. I've often heard people say, "If I could just catch a break and get a platform like that, I could make a difference." I've even been guilty of saying that many times myself. The media has deceived us into thinking we can only make a difference in the world if we have the "big name" to go with the big platform. I believe this is a lie from the enemy, and I'm here to tell you otherwise. Having this mentality taints the way we think about ourselves. We use a worldly measuring stick to see if we, along with our stories, are qualified. The one thing we forget is the scale that is put in place by God is the only one that determines our destiny. You don't have to be a superstar to shine. All you need to be is a willing and obedient vessel available to be used by your Father. And by the way, you already have the name, because you come from the bloodline of Jesus.

There are numerous examples in Scripture of people with platforms who were used by God to do mighty things. Many of them were ordinary people, just like us. If we were living out their story, we probably wouldn't see the huge platforms we sometimes chase in the moment. Instead, I think we would see a loving God using any platform necessary to showcase His glory. We'd probably see the most unqualified people as the vessels, as well. Let's take a look at a variety of men and women who had platforms of all shapes and sizes who were used by God.

ABRAHAM – An old man who became a father
Once people get into their forties, usually having children is far from their mind, for multiple reasons. However, when Abraham was 100 years old, his wife, Sarah, bore him a son, Isaac, just as God had promised (Genesis 21). God's covenant with Abraham would be fulfilled through Isaac. He went on to become the father of Israel and ultimately the modern Jewish nation. It was through Isaac's lineage that Jesus the Messiah was born.

JOSEPH – A young dreamer who led a nation
The story of Joseph (Genesis 37) is one of my favorites, because I feel I can relate so well to him. He had a dream given to him by God as a seventeen year old, and instead of beginning to walk out that dream as he imagined he would, he went through a bunch of what seemed like detours, and his life ended up looking a lot different than I'm sure he had imagined. However, at the age of thirty, he became second-in-command to Pharaoh and saw his dream become reality. While most of us have never been sold into slavery or wrongfully imprisoned, we have had life go much differently than we imagined, seemingly in the opposite direction of the dreams God once placed in our heart.

GIDEON – A military leader and judge
In the book of Judges, we learn Gideon was the fifth judge over Israel. He is introduced in the sixth chapter of Judges while

collecting wheat and hiding it from the enemy. An angel came to him and asked him to take on the task of overthrowing the Midianites. As a leader of the Israelites, he won a decisive victory over a Midianite army despite a vast numerical disadvantage, leading a troop of three hundred valiant men to victory.

RAHAB - A prostitute
Rahab was one of the most unlikely people ever to be used by God (Joshua 2). She was a prostitute living in Jericho, who provided refuge for the Israelite spies when they went to scout out the town and its surrounding areas. Even though the King of Jericho commanded the men be brought out to him so they could be punished, she hid them; and as a result, God spared her and her family when the Israelites entered the town and overthrew it.

JONAH - A man who ran from God
Jonah was a prophet who was called by God to go and minister to the people of Nineveh. These people were considered to be godless, so Jonah was instructed to tell the people God's judgment was coming against them. Because of how wicked they were, Jonah didn't want to go to Nineveh, so he ran from God. This resulted in him being swallowed by a large fish. While he was in the belly of the fish, Jonah prayed to God for forgiveness and protection; and as a result, God gave him a second chance and spared the people of Nineveh, since they repented just like Jonah.

A LITTLE BOY - A key player in the miracle of two fish and five loaves
Jesus always fed the hungry. So when He saw a crowd of five thousand people (John 6), it was business as usual. He asked His disciples to find food for the people, and they returned with a

little boy's lunch. Jesus turned the two fish and five loaves into a miraculous meal feeding five thousand men, not counting the women and children.

THE WOMAN AT THE WELL – An adulterous Samaritan

In John 4, the story of a woman that Jesus meets at a well is remarkable. Jesus, being a Jew, wasn't even supposed to talk to her, as she was a Samaritan. The culture of that day meant Jews did not associate with Samaritans. It was definitely a no no for men to talk to women in public at that time, as well. Women were regarded as private property. Not only did Jesus talk to her, He ministered to her. After her encounter with the Messiah, she left her belongings at the well and told everyone about Him. She became a missionary in Samaria. Because of her testimony, many people believed.

Many times God uses unlikely and ordinary people to do great things. He also uses simple platforms to make an impact. As we just read in a few examples, He used both men and women of all ages and from all walks of life to do His work. Some were on very large platforms, but some were not. No matter where they were in their life, they allowed God to use them. We are all part of the body of Christ, and He uses us in different ways to make the body complete. Focus on the here and now, not on tomorrow or where you want to go next year. If you become who you are called to be in the now, you will be where you are meant to be in the future.

I think of our platforms much like a fingerprint. No two fingerprints are the same. Our hands may look like everyone else's, but the fine details of our fingerprints are extremely different than any other. Your platform is unique, and only you possess it. Your platform is also important, so use it.

Maybe your platform doesn't currently look like what you think it should, but it is significant in the eyes of the Lord. You very well may be exactly where He wants you in the now. You influence the people who see you every day, and you have a role to play in their lives. So whether your circle of influence consists of a few friends at school, followers on social media, kids who look up to you as a parent, a spouse who watches your every move, a few employees who answer to you, some teammates on a sports team, or a large group of people who see you regularly for various reasons, YOU HAVE A PLATFORM. You are responsible for that platform. What you do on and with your platform now will be very evident to everyone later. Your current platform may or may not one day lead to a larger platform. We have to remember no matter where our platforms—big and small—take us, we can make a difference.

"A platform is a tool God gives us humans to use for making Him famous. The size, shape, and nature of the platform vary based on our individual calling."

Keith Stancil
President of Artist Garden Entertainment, Author of *CREATING MONSTERS*

A WORD FROM THE CHURCH...

By Brian Scoggin, drummer for GRAMMY® and Dove Award winning band Casting Crowns

Along my journey of faith in Christ I have seen God expand my influence for His kingdom simply by continuing to "seek first His kingdom." When I take the time to look back at God's goodness to me over the years, it's then that I realize all the ways God has provided for and prepared me to be right where He has me now. There have been times when my platform wasn't very visible, but I still had the responsibility to bloom there. Faithfulness in small things is an indicator of how we'll handle big things. (Luke 16:10)

Every opportunity that's ever come my way hasn't been because I was seeking it. Opportunities always came in a season when I was simply seeking God. Being faithful where you're planted will always catch the eye of those God will use to extend new opportunities to you. Realizing and accepting the influence and responsibilities which God has entrusted you with now will keep you from yearning for those just out of reach. Don't miss out on the present. God is moving and expanding His kingdom through the "day in, day out" routine of faithfulness in the small things.

TODAY'S CHALLENGE

Choose to make the most of your current platform. Embrace where you are right now. Grow where you are planted. You may not think you are an influencer, but you are. God has called you to make an eternal impact. Take a minute and think about what your platform looks like and how you can make a difference for Him with it.

1) **Read Genesis 41:41-57.**

2) **Write down a description of your platform and place it somewhere you will see it every day to remind you where God has placed you as an influencer in this season of your life.**

3) **Write down your strongest gifts on the same paper.**

4) **Go to those in your circle of influence, and use one of your gifts to encourage, help, or share Christ with them.**

PRAYER

God, I ask that You help reveal what my platform and gifts are to me. I know You want to use both for Your glory, so please help me be obedient and aware of how You want to use my platform today. In Jesus' name, amen.

DAY 5:
YOUR TIME

"For whatever one sows, that will he also reap."

Galatians 6:7 (ESV)

"

IS WHAT YOU'RE
GETTING WORTH
WHAT YOU'RE
GIVING UP?

— UNKNOWN

DAY 5:

YOUR TIME

Having children is a huge blessing. If you have them, you know all about the treasure that a child is to a parent. My wife and I have two boys. Our oldest, Samuel, who is the spitting image of the Energizer Bunny, is 4 years old. Our youngest, Ezekiel ("Zeek"), was born in 2016. My boys have taught me a lot about life, about God, about love, and even how to use a razor to shave my head since most of my hair has fallen out. You can find me on Facebook (@noahclevelandmusic) to see pictures proving I actually had hair before kids. The love I have for them is beyond explanation or even comprehension, and nothing will ever change the love I have for them. One thing I am learning, still, is how to love them.

One of the greatest books I've ever read is The Five Love Languages, by Gary Chapman. In his book, he states we all communicate and feel loved through various ways or "languages." Every human has what he calls a "love tank," and only certain actions of love fill that tank up. What may fill your tank up might be completely different from the person sitting next to you. Some feel loved by words of affirmation, some by receiving gifts, some by physical touch, some by acts of service, and some by quality time. How is your love tank filled? You might feel loved by more than one.

It quickly became evident to me that my oldest son's love languages were receiving gifts and quality time. When I return home from a ministry trip that he didn't go on or even running simple errands around town, Samuel always lights up if I bring him a gift. It doesn't matter what it is; for him, it's just the fact that Daddy brought him a gift and filled up his love tank. His other love language is quality time. Spending time together for him is magical. Again, it's not what we are doing, but it's the fact that it's being done together.

This year I took Samuel on our first annual "guys only trip." When we travel doing ministry, almost all of our time is accounted for by serving others, so I intentionally planned some time for just the two of us. His favorite thing to do together is play golf, so we started the trip off on the golf course. After a few hours swinging the clubs, we checked in at a hotel and got ready for dinner. At the restaurant, we sat side by side rather than across from each other, and he hugged me more in that forty-five minute time period than I could ever remember him hugging me. I could tell the quality time I was spending with him was filling up his love tank. We finished the night off with a movie called Wall-E, cuddled up in bed, eating Finding Nemo popcorn. The next morning we hit the continental breakfast downstairs (one of his hotel must haves,) and headed to an arcade dressed as super heroes. The bonding between us on this trip was priceless and revealed many things to me. I realized through revelation from the Holy Spirit, that no matter where we are or what we do, the whole world is right for him when Daddy and Samuel are together. I pray I will always remember this, especially as we both get older.

Time is something most of us have little of, and if we do possess it, there's not much quality in it. We use it to gain ground in our lives or careers or to advance to the next step no matter what it costs us. The world we live in has no margins or limits. In the most chaotic moments, if something needs to be done, we find the time even if it is borrowed from some other place in our lives. But what happens when we've taken more than we can give back? What happens to our relationships when we're working off borrowed time? In many instances, we keep the train rolling down the tracks toward greatness and gain for ourselves, and in doing so, that takes precedence. We make time for those late night emails. We make time for late meetings that cause us to miss dinner or miss putting our kids to bed. We use our "day(s) off" to work overtime. We work tirelessly on the Sabbath. If you're like me, you're guilty of all of the above, among other things.

In fact, I have a confession to make. I have often traded Samuel's quality time for personal gain. Jesus said in Matthew 16:26, "What good will it be for a man if he gains the whole world, yet loses his soul?" We chase dreams, profit, and progress; and we lose sight of one of our most valuable assets—time. God has challenged me in a healthy way to place margins in my life that will allow me to make the most of my time with my family. Richard Swenson said it best in his book, *Margins*:

"How might we know that the relational environments are where God would have us concentrate? Simply put, these are the same areas Christ spent his TIME developing and where His teaching is focused."

If Jesus spent much of His time investing in relationships, how much more focus should we put into ours?

Many times when I talk to people who are older and wiser than me, and who have been very successful in life, I'll ask them this question: "What is your biggest regret?" The answer has almost been unanimous. Most say they wish they had spent more time with their family. I asked one man this question recently, and his answer is tattooed on my soul forever:

"I was the father who was at every sporting event, every vacation, and every school function. The problem was I was always on the phone building my business and chasing success. The only thing on my mind was how to make the next dollar. I was present with my family, but in essence, I wasn't even there. My little girl would always ask me to take her fishing, but I was too busy. I thought I had plenty of time to make it up to her. I finally realized what I had missed when she was around fifteen years old. The only problem at that moment was it was too late, and I had run out of time. At this point, I was the one asking her to go fishing, but she wasn't interested anymore. I missed those moments because of how I managed my time. So son, please remember, one day time may not be on your side, so use it wisely while it still is."

Wow! You can imagine the tears that rolled down his face and mine after he told me this. I was simply asking advice, but the conviction and pain that poured out from this man left a lasting impact on me. It was his story, but it hit me right square in the middle of mine. It ministered to me in a way that few things ever have. It challenged me to put a priority on my time with those I love. It showed me how little margin I've had in my life. Sometimes it can be hard and very challenging to take time out of our busy lives to give to someone else, but the fruits of our time now will be evident to everyone down the road, including ourselves.

A WORD FROM THE CHURCH...

By Sheila Weed, Hospice Care Administrator

I manage a hospice that has at-home patients, as well as a twelve-bed in-patient unit. It can be a challenge to manage my time amidst the busyness of a demanding work schedule. Everyone needs me at once: my employees, the patients in the home, the patients in the unit, family members of these patients, the director of nursing, and my boss. For me, the key to balancing it all is something I ask the Lord to help me with constantly, and that's to manage my time wisely.

I have to ask myself, "What is the most important task for me to spend my energy on right now?" That is followed by, "Who should I help, or what is next?" Every day I aim to move through my schedule using these questions. Sometimes I just have to stop and ask God to reveal to me what the priorities should be, because I want to serve everyone. Do I miss the mark at times? Of course I do; but through each entire day of chaos, I can see God's plan being carried out when He uses me to touch the lives of hurting, and many times, dying people.

"To everything there is a season and a time to every purpose under the heavens: a time to be born and a time to die, a time to plant and a time to pluck up that which is planted, a time to kill and a time to heal, a time to break down and a time to build up, a time to weep, and a time to laugh, a time to mourn and a time to dance." (Ecclesiastes 3:1-4, KJV)

TODAY'S CHALLENGE

Who are the people you love the most in your life? I'm sure you have family members who need your time. They just need you to be there. You may even have close friends who could even use some quality time with you.

1) **Read Luke 22:14-20.** Notice what Jesus is doing right before He is arrested and sent to the cross. He is spending time with His disciples. He shares a meal with them in fellowship and has communion. Fellowship is something Jesus instilled in His disciples, to the point where they devoted themselves to it. (Acts 2:42)

2) **Invite a family member(s) or close friend(s) that you need to spend quality time with to hang out.** Maybe it's a meal, a movie, a sporting event, etc. Spend this time with them strategically by loving them, encouraging them, laughing with them, and making the time about them, and not you.

PRAYER

God, I thank You for my family and friends. Fellowship with people comes from You, and these relationships are also from You. Help me make this time of fellowship look the way You want it to look. If there are things I need to say, please give me the words to use. Let Your Holy Spirit guide me during this time. In Jesus' name, amen.

DAY 6:
PRAYER

"And they devoted themselves to the apostles' teaching and the fellowship, to the breaking of bread and the prayers."

Acts 2:42 (ESV)

"

TALKING TO MEN
FOR GOD IS A GREAT
THING, BUT TALKING
TO GOD FOR MEN IS
GREATER STILL.

— E.M. BOUNDS

DAY 6:

PRAYER

Has it ever been hard for you to pray? I don't mean the blessing at dinnertime, although that may be a challenge for you, too. I mean, has it ever been hard for you to *really* pray for someone or something? There are 650 prayers listed in the Bible. Twenty-five are recorded from Jesus during His earthly ministry. The Bible lists nine main types of prayer:

1. Prayer of Faith (James 5:15)

2. Corporate Prayer (Acts 2:42)

3. Prayer of Petition and Supplication (Philippians 4:6)

4. Prayer of Thanksgiving (Psalms 95:2-3)

5. Prayer of Worship (Acts 13:2-3)

6. Prayer of Consecration (Matthew 26:39)

7. Prayer of Intercession (1 Timothy 2:1)

8. Prayer of Salvation (Psalms 69)

9. Praying In The Spirit (1 Corinthians 14:14-15)

Prayer is vital to the life of any believer, as it's our line of communication to the Father. Before Jesus said, "It is finished" on the cross, only a chosen mediator could communicate with

God. Everyone else had to wait until the designated person heard from God, and then that person would share what God said with everyone. In Exodus 25, God commanded Moses to build a tabernacle, which contained an inner room specifically to be God's special dwelling place to meet and communicate with Him. Within this Holy Place, there was a curtain known as the veil, which separated the dwelling place called the Holy of Holies from the rest of the room. In Hebrew the word veil means a screen or divider. The veil was used as a picture or symbol to describe a barrier between man and God. This curtain was essentially used to separate a holy God from sinful man. No ordinary man could enter this sacred space, as entering the Holy of Holies meant entering the very presence of God. In fact, anyone who entered besides the high priest would die. Even the high priest only went in once a year (Hebrews 9:7).

The presence of God remained shielded from man behind a thick curtain throughout the history of Israel. However, the death of Jesus on the cross changed all of this for mankind forever. When He died, the curtain in Jerusalem was torn in half from top to bottom (Matthew 27:51). The death of Jesus meant atonement for our sins, which made us right before God. There was no longer a need for that barrier, as our sins were forgiven and we had direct access to God.

We can now boldly enter into God's presence, "the inner sanctuary behind the curtain, where Jesus, who went before us, has entered on our behalf" (Hebrews 6:19-22). If the veil was torn, and we have direct access to God, why don't we use our access more?

> We can now boldly enter into God's presence.

I used to think of myself as someone who prayed, before coming to the painful conclusion that I wasn't exactly a prayer warrior. This revelation came to me when my wife handed me a book called *The Power of a Praying Husband*, by Stormie Omartian. She told me she had just finished reading *The Power of a Praying Wife* by this same author, and the book was life-changing for her.

My first instinct was to be offended, feeling like my wife didn't think I prayed enough. I thought to myself, *Are there things in my life that wave a red flag at her? I mean, come on; I am a Christian artist and speaker, who sings and preaches about Jesus, so don't you think I know how to pray?* I love my wife dearly and always want our relationship to grow, so I agreed to read it. I had no idea how it would change me.

First of all, if you are a husband, this book *will* change your life, so I recommend you go buy it now and read it. Stormie paints a picture in a perfect way to help men understand how women tick and answers some questions you've probably asked many times either out loud or in your head. It is like getting a magazine full of cheat codes for those video games you could never beat growing up. Understanding how my wife thought about me, why she did or said certain things, and what she really desired of me in many situations, was mind-blowing and life-altering.

At the end of every chapter, there was a list of things for me to pray about for my wife. So I started a prayer list that I still use today. Chapter after chapter produced prayer after prayer, some straight from the book and some from me personally. What was so incredible was I could see praying for my wife was actually working in a powerful way in real time. The funny thing was, many of the prayers didn't result in her changing, but me changing.

Praying for her was in a lot of ways praying for me. After all, we are one so this is the way it works right?

It is still very evident when I don't pray for my wife daily. My attitude stinks up the whole house. I am short with her, rude, rough, selfish, and so out of touch with her needs. My wife can tell as well, but she never brings up the fact she knows I am not praying; but I know she knows. The way I act can affect my prayers in a great way as stated in 1 Peter 3:7, ESV: "Likewise, husbands, live with your wives in an understanding way, showing honor to the woman as the weaker vessel, since they are heirs with you of the grace of life, so that your prayers may not be hindered."

> "Whatever you don't pray about in your life you leave up to chance."
> **- Stormie Omartian**
> Author of *THE POWER OF A PRAYING HUSBAND*

I once heard a pastor say at a marriage conference, "Wherever your wife is, you've led her there." Ouch! That's a tough one to swallow. I have found this to be so true in my life though, and in my prayers for my wife, as well. As a husband, I am the leader of my house. My first and foremost calling, after my relationship with God, is to my wife. She is under my leadership, and it's my job to blanket her with my prayers. I know there are many people who pray for her, but as her husband and soulmate, my prayers are different. They come from a different place. She desperately needs my prayers as much as she needs me.

I want to challenge you today to pray. Don't only pray for yourself, but pray for someone else. When we become aware of the souls who are around us, we can truly make an impact.

I have found it much easier to pray for my desires and dreams than someone else's. The words seem to flow a little more clearly and faster when it's about me. But praying for someone else and their needs can be more difficult. Praying for someone else is a selfless act. It causes us to serve and takes our minds off of ourselves for a little while. There are days that I have to get out of my own way to pray for my wife, children, and others for whom God has led me to pray. You may be like I was and think you know how to pray, but take some time to honestly ask yourself if this is, in fact, true. Hold a mirror up to your prayer life today. What do you see? What does it consist of? Are your prayers focused solely on you and your desires? Are your prayers for other people? Or does your prayer life simply consist of the occasional, "God is great. God is good. Let us thank Him for our food." When we tap into true prayer, it often reveals how little we actually prayed previously. How many changes have you seen that resulted from your prayers? Prayer can alter circumstances, but it can also change you. Ultimately, we have to pray for God's will to be done in every situation above all, so prayer is far from a genie in a bottle. However, we've seen in Scripture that God does hear our prayers, and according to His will, He answers them.

There have been many instances where my prayers didn't get answered, or at least they weren't answered to my knowledge. Some may have been answered with a beautiful "yes," some with a resounding "no," and still there are some prayers I may never know the answer, because it was for someone else. Being consistent in our prayer life is vital to who we are in Christ. When it's absent from our walk with Him, it's like going to war without a weapon. This is why Paul ends his awesome sermon on the armor of God by warning us spiritual soldiers that we must "pray at all times in the Spirit, with all prayer and supplication" (Ephesians 6:18).

There's really no magic formula for a dynamic prayer life, we just have to make it a priority in our busy lives. So whether you're praying for a situation in your life today or for someone else's, be persistent. Pray from your heart, not from your head. Don't leave the results up to chance, step in and let your requests be made known to God (Philippians 4:6).

A WORD FROM THE CHURCH...
By Holly Starr, National Recording Artist

There isn't a perfect formula for prayer. But just like working out, the more we exercise those muscles, the easier it is to lift the "heavy stuff." I have found that my prayer life directly impacts the way I respond to life's ups and downs. If I have been faithful in prayer, it's easier to trust God when something unexpected or troubling happens. If I haven't been faithful in prayer, it's a whole lot harder!

One day in high school, I was working in the library putting away some books when I had an epiphany about prayer. I remember thinking, I can talk to God right here, right now...about whatever I'm wondering, worried, or excited about! I had always heard prayer was just like talking to God, but in that moment, I realized for the first time just how close He was to me on a moment-by-moment basis. It was amazing! From that point on, I began to explore prayer and how to do it well. In fact, I'm still exploring it!

A camp counselor once taught me a way to pray represented by the acronym "ACTS"—Adoration, Confession, Thanksgiving, and Supplication. This method stretched my prayer life in a great way! Praying in this order taught me how to remember WHO I'm talking to (Adoration – taking time to remember/adore who God is), then what He did for me (Confession – taking time to confess any sin I had committed, big or small), followed by expressing gratitude for His provision in my life (Thanksgiving), and concluding with my prayer requests I might have (Supplication).

Prior to learning this prayer habit, I found myself always praying for what I wanted or needed first, taking little time to thank Him, confess my wrongdoings, or adore who He is—all very important things! When I started putting His will first, and humbling myself before Him with my weaknesses, my requests weren't as desperate as they once were, but instead, filled with trust in the Creator of my soul and His perfect timing. Wow! What an amazing privilege to carry everything to God in prayer.

TODAY'S CHALLENGE

You may or may not have a spouse to pray for, but regardless, there are people in your life who desperately need your prayers. This challenge may be difficult for some of you, as you may not be as comfortable praying as others are, but be encouraged because "you can do all things through Christ who strengthens you." (Philippians 4:13)

1) **Read Exodus 32:1-14.** Notice how Moses prayed and interceded on behalf of the children of Israel. God was very angry with them and ready to destroy them until Moses prayed and changed God's mind.

2) **Write five people's names down, and pray for each person individually.**

3) **Find one person to pray out loud with.** This prayer doesn't have to be super long or spiritual. A good way to initiate this is to simply ask the Holy Spirit to lead you to the right person, and then ask them if they would be comfortable if you prayed for them. Maybe even ask them if they have any specific things they would like you to pray with them about.

PRAYER

God, thank You for the opportunity to talk to You myself. This open line of communication is extremely vital to my spiritual life. I ask that You lead me to the right person today and that I would have the courage and boldness to pray with them out loud. Your power is made perfect in my weakness. In Jesus' name, amen.

DAY 7:
GIVING

"So WHEN you give to the needy..."

Matthew 6:2 (ESV)

"

THE WORLD ASKS,
'WHAT DOES
A MAN OWN?'
CHRIST ASKS,
'HOW DOES
HE USE IT?'

— ANDREW MURRAY

GIVING

Giving is contagious. The moment we give, we don't just meet the need of the person we give to, we create a ripple effect felt way down the line by others. A study by James Fowler of the University of California, San Diego, and Nicholas Christakis of Harvard University, published in the *Proceedings of the National Academy of Science*, shows when one person behaves generously now, it inspires observers to be generous later on, toward different people. In fact, the researchers found "each person in a network can influence dozens or even hundreds of people, some of whom he or she does not know or ever meet."

We can give many things to help others, but I want us to focus on money. Jesus talked about money a lot. In fact, He mentioned money more than He did heaven and hell combined. Eleven of the thirty-nine parables record Him talking about finances. It's crazy to think Jesus mentioned money more than love, but when you study the Scriptures, you will find it is true.

I grew up hearing a lot about love, heaven, and hell, so to see money was mentioned more than all those intrigued me greatly. As I studied this, it made me wonder why. I figured I needed to pay close attention to it if Jesus talked about it so much. Could it be He is interested in our money more than anything else? Absolutely not! I believe He knew more of us would struggle with our spending habits than many other things in our lives. This world is filled with people living paycheck to paycheck, in debt up to their necks, so there has to be something that lies beneath the surface of His reasoning.

Before He started His ministry, Jesus was a carpenter, so I'm sure He knew it took money to live. Yet, we have numerous examples where He shows us the value we place on money is far from what it should be in our lives. We see this when He called young men to be His disciples and to leave everything they had behind and follow Him. He certainly had to be convincing, because they took nothing with them. If they were trying to start a fishing company, tax company, or construction company, it didn't matter; because they left it all behind just to follow a man who didn't have a bank account or even a place to lay His head.

Peter was a fisherman when he came in contact with Jesus. His livelihood depended on him catching fish, but when he caught the biggest load of fish of his career, he "left everything and followed Him" (Luke 5:11). His load of fish would have brought him more money, food, and even notoriety than he had ever experienced before, yet he left it all behind. Maybe he saw in that moment there was more to life than money, and if this was a sign of things to come, he was all in.

Jesus would say things like, "Do not worry about your life, what you will eat or drink; or about your body or what you will wear" (Matthew 6:25 NIV). I'm sure the world shouted things to these disciples just like it shouts to us: "Save all you can! Get it while the getting is good! They're just trying to get your money! You've worked too hard for this to give it away! They're the ones who made the mistake, so why should you help?" But Jesus said in Matthew 6:19-20, ESV "Do not lay up for yourselves treasures on earth, where moth and rust destroy and where thieves break in and steal, but lay up for yourselves treasures in heaven, where neither moth nor rust destroys and where thieves do not break in and steal. For where your treasure is, there your heart will be also."

One thing I've noticed when looking at the life of Jesus, was how He was always the exact opposite image of the world. When the world said, "take," Jesus said, "give." When the world said, "hate," Jesus showed love. When the world said they were sick, Jesus said, "Be healed." In many instances, we hear Jesus say something like, "You've heard it said this way, but I'm going to say it different." Over and over in the Gospels, He represented something different than what the world portrayed. When it came to giving, it was never a question of whether or not to give; it was a question of how. Oftentimes, it looked like Him giving everything. When it comes to our giving, we need to remember what Jesus said and not focus on what the world tells us.

Money reveals who we are. Jesus compared money to a master when He said, "You cannot serve both God and money" (Matthew 6:24, ESV). For many of us, money can become a master. It becomes a master when every decision we make is based on the dollar amount. It's our master when every step in our journey revolves around it, when we wake up and think every day how to serve it. Most of the time it starts ruling our lives without us even knowing it's in charge. We become a slave to it but can't see the chains enslaving us.

"For the love of money is a root for all kinds of evil. Some people, eager for money, have wandered from the faith and pierced themselves with many griefs." (1 Timothy 6:10, NIV)

That root makes us do things we would never do otherwise. In many instances, money equals power. Everyone wants to be

CHURCH WITH NO WALLS: A 21-DAY CHALLENGE

powerful, and the key to that power is money. So most people think if you have enough money, you can have anything in this world you want.

I believe we can easily see whether or not money is our master based on where it goes. There's an old saying, "Put your money where your mouth is." The things we are most interested in and invested in get our money, plain and simple. If we are serious about something, we invest. I think this is what Jesus was talking about when He said our heart would be where our treasure is.

Who and what do we give our money to? When we move beyond everyday essentials and our monthly bills, we see the proof right there in the pudding. What's left? God tells us in Malachi 3 that our tithe of ten percent is to go to the storehouse, and in our case, that is our home church.

> ## "No one has ever become poor by giving."
> **- Anne Frank**
> Author of *THE DIARY OF A YOUNG GIRL*

At the end of the year when doing the dreaded task of taxes, I am reminded of what my wife and I have given from our personal and ministry accounts the previous year. Numbers don't lie, and we have to answer the question ourselves—who is our master? The proof on paper tells us where we spent our treasure. We will see what our tithes look like, as well as our offerings.

Now please don't misunderstand what I'm trying to say here. We are not looking to exceed a certain number in giving, per se, in order to get a pat on the back; but at the same time, we know how our ministry operates and what it should look like based on God's instruction to us in our giving. As a ministry, we have a missions budget that we use to give to other ministries, families in need, missionaries, and other things God leads us to give to over the course of the year. After implementing this practice a few years ago, we found that time after time throughout the year, God would send us people who needed our giving. Our task in this matter is simply to pray and ask God to lead us to those in need and then be obedient. Sometimes we are stretched beyond what we think we have, but obedience is always greater than sacrifice (1 Samuel 15:22).

I have a few great mentors in my life who are very wealthy, and they have all told me on different occasions, "It's just money." If these wealthy men believe that, then there has to be some wisdom and freedom in those words. These men are some of the most generous men I've ever encountered. The value they put on giving far outweighs the value they put on the dollar amount. What value do you put on money?

I encourage you to look at your budget from the past few months and see where your money has gone. What have you spent it on? What percentage do you see beside giving ? Do you see a reflection of a generous person in your statements? Are you a giving person based on what you see? If not, then it's time to ask yourself why not. If Jesus mentioned money more than anything else, shouldn't we be very aware of what we do with it? When I get to heaven one day, I will have to give an account for all the resources (Romans 14:12) that came my way, and my prayer is that I will not have used it all trying to build my own kingdom, but His Kingdom.

A WORD FROM THE CHURCH...
By Jerry Thomas, Army Veteran

You may have heard the story about the widow's offering. How after many rich people put in large amounts of money into the temple treasury, a poor widow put in two copper coins worth only a few cents. Jesus commented that the others gave out of their wealth, but she gave everything she had to live on (Mark 12:41-44).

Many people walk out their lives with Christ in the same way. Some talk about Christ, and others have some minimal level of involvement with the Church. However, some have admittedly not made a complete commitment to Christ in every aspect of their lives. We should give our money, but more importantly, ourselves—wholly and completely—to the cause of God.

TODAY'S CHALLENGE

When we seek the Kingdom of God first, everything else falls into place. (Matthew 6:33) This is one of the laws of the Kingdom. Galatians 6:7 says, "A man reaps what he sows." That tells me if I sow an apple seed, I'll reap an apple, right? If I sow an orange seed, should I expect a watermelon? Of course not! In the same manner, when we sow money, we can expect to reap money. If there is no seed in the ground, then we should not be expecting to receive a harvest. It's not God's intent for us to give only so we can receive. This concept, given to us in the Scriptures (Galatians 6:7), is the law of seedtime and harvest, promising it will come back. If we are to reap what we sow, then it's not a matter of if, but when it comes back.

1) **Read Malachi 3:6-12.**

2) **Read Matthew 6:2-4.**

3) **Find someone to give money to.** This can be a church, a ministry, a missionary, a preacher, or just someone in need. Ask God to reveal the recipient of this gift and the exact number that you are to give.

PRAYER

God, thank You for all You've given me. I know everything I have belongs to You. Give me the faith to be a giver. Change my heart to be a giver. I don't want to be bound by the chains of greed or allow money to be my master. You are my God and King, and I owe everything to You. Now, please reveal to me how much I am to give today and where it needs to go. I pray also that my seed falls onto fertile soil and makes an impact for the Kingdom of God. In Jesus' name, amen.

DAY 8:

FASTING

"And WHEN you fast..."

Matthew 6:16 [ESV]

"

FASTING IS A GRACE THAT SIGNIFICANTLY INCREASES OUR RECEPTIVITY TO THE LORD'S VOICE AND HIS WORD.

— MIKE BICKLE

DAY 8:

FASTING

Going without food is just plain hard. If you've ever been to the doctor or hospital, and they tell you to be on an all-liquid diet for twenty-four hours before you come back for surgery or a procedure, you know what I'm talking about. You immediately get unsettled and think you may not make it to the appointment because of starvation.

Our body needs food, so when it doesn't get it, it gives us serious hunger pains. I love the Snickers commercials on television that say we aren't ourselves when we are hungry. My wife tells me I get "hangry" in the moments when I get really hungry. I hate to admit it, but I probably do act a little different when I need food.

Have you ever fasted before? *The New Oxford American Dictionary* defines fasting as "abstaining from all or some kinds of food or drink, especially as a religious observance."

I've often taken time away and "fasted" from social media, secular music, television, and even sports for various reasons. While I think healthy results can come from abstaining from those things, they don't represent biblical fasting. Based on the core definition, abstaining from food or drink is how I am to fast. It is one of the most demanding things a follower of Jesus can do to his or her body. Why would God ask us to not eat? If our body needs food, shouldn't we just give it what it needs? Well, I think that's the whole purpose behind it. God knows for us to go without food is a great sacrifice, especially when we switch our focus to Him during that time.

The Bible is full of stories where men and women of God fasted. Some were filled with short fasts, and some were filled with long fasts. One story even consisted of every living being, including animals, going without food (Jonah 3:7). One common denominator in all of the stories of fasting we read about in the Bible was fasting was always for a spiritual purpose. We view fasting as a physical act, but it is really a spiritual act. The idea behind it is to replace the craving we have for food with a craving for God's presence. It's a sacrifice that replaces our will and desire with God's will and desire. Instead of focusing on food, we turn our focus on Jesus. When those hunger pains are at their max, clinging to God is the quencher. Jesus even told us in Matthew 16:24, ESV, "If anyone would come after me, he must deny himself." Fasting is the very definition of denying ourselves, right? We as Christians want to believe we follow and emulate Christ, but many of us have never fasted at all. Jesus also said in Matthew 6:16, "And when you fast," which tells me He was referring to something happening with regularity based on the word *when*. In this day and age, fasting is obsolete in the lives of most believers. It's easy to find ways to shrug off the notion of fasting anytime we hear about it or when we feel prompted to practice it. Many churches do corporate fasts, which can be a very powerful ritual.

Before He started His ministry, Jesus went into the wilderness and fasted for forty days and forty nights (Matthew 4). During this time, He ate nothing. Satan came and tempted Him when He was at His weakest, but He turned to the Father and used His Word to fight off every temptation. Obviously, the Son of God saw a need to fast, so it might be a wise practice for me to consider as well. I have found in my walk with Christ there's no method to fasting, but only sensitivity of how and when.

The disciples had power and authority given to them by Jesus, but there was one instance where they

"When you fast, your spirit becomes uncluttered by the things of this world and amazingly sensitive to the things of God. Once you've experienced even a glimpse of this and the countless rewards and blessings that follow, it changes your entire perspective."

Jentezen Franklin
Pastor of Free Chapel
Gainesville, GA

encountered an evil spirit in a young boy that they could not drive out. Jesus comes on the scene and drives the evil spirit out, so the disciples later ask Him why they couldn't do it. He says, "This kind can come out by nothing but prayer and fasting" (Mark 9:29, NKJV). So does fasting activate power? I think the obvious answer is yes. Without a doubt, power is missing from our churches, mainly because the leaders of the church feel no need to model fasting for their congregations. Some say it's a personal practice, and while that is very true, people need an example to follow. They need to be led, and when there's no one leading or teaching it, there's no response. Response comes after revelation. The church I was saved at and grew up in never taught, mentioned, or encouraged fasting to my knowledge. When fasting is absent in our lives, I believe other things are as well.

The same Spirit who raised Jesus from the grave lives inside of us (Romans 8:11). We as His followers have a power and anointing, but many times, we taint it with our own sin and selfishness. When there is too much of us, we have a problem. Our spiritual balance gets out of sync. Our prayer needs to be "more of Him and less of us."

The evidence of "less of us" is one thing we can guarantee will be accomplished when we fast. We become more aware of Jesus in our lives and situations. Fasting allows us to rid ourselves of selfishness. It also allows us to see and hear Him with more clarity, and in essence, become more aware of God in all aspects of our lives.

God has called me to fast for many different things. Some have been for my family, our ministry, my church, or myself; and some have been for other people. I have been led by God to do a one-day fast, and I have been led by God to do all the way up to a twenty-one day fast. My wife and I always do some sort of fast at the beginning of the year as we seek God's direction for our ministry and life together for the upcoming year. The clarity we receive from God during these times is so powerful and revealing. There are even times when we are seeking God for an answer or for a certain direction, and going into a time of fasting seems to always help gain understanding in those situations. God has spoken great revelations during my fasts that I know I would have never received otherwise.

One day when I was a freshman in college, God spoke to me to fast for my roommate, Jason. We were about to leave for Christmas break, and God urged me to do a three-day fast for him and his finances. He was in need of a miracle. He needed $5,000 to pay his tuition, or he would not be able to return for the second semester. So as our holiday break began, I stayed in the dorm a few extra days to fast for him and pray. He had no idea.

After the three days ended, I left for home. A week or so later, I got a call from Jason and he said, "You'll never guess what just happened... I just received a $5,000 check for my tuition." All I could do was laugh, shout, and celebrate with him. He was so excited to be able to come back after our Christmas break, and I was honored to share that moment with him. This was one of the first times I had ever fasted, but I knew right then that there was power in being obedient when it came to fasting.

Scripture tells us fasting should be a part of every believer's life, but it takes a lot of discipline to deny our own physical need for food. However, it's worth saying again, if the Son of Man fasted, then it's a good idea for us to follow suit.

A WORD FROM THE CHURCH...
By Christian Nichles, Family Life Pastor at First Baptist Church Moss Bluff in Lake Charles, LA

It's interesting what Jesus says in Matthew 6:16: "and *WHEN* you fast..." Jesus is prescriptively commanding that His people fast and then encouraging their process. The Church today is, without a doubt, in need of a fresh move of God. The spiritual anemia across western Christendom is evident. Perhaps, if we the Church would make fasting an integral part of our spiritual walk, small group process, and worship gatherings, revival would come. Maybe, just maybe, we would experience a fresh move of God that would seminally shift our churches, our culture, and our world!

TODAY'S CHALLENGE

Remember, fasting is not intended for you to starve yourself but to help you become more aware of God's presence in your life. Fasting will help you have clarity about things which may have been foggy before. It's also not something we shout from the rooftops either. Even when fasting is corporate, with a body of believers joining together at the same time, it's still very much a private matter between you and God.

1) **Read Daniel 10:1-14.**

2) **Ask God how He would want you to fast today.** Maybe it's a sun-up to sun-down fast. Maybe it's one meal. Maybe it's all day. But whatever God tells you, be obedient to Him. Whatever meal or meals you feel led to fast today, take time and pray. After your fast is over, reflect and be aware of what God did in you. Ask God to reveal things to you from the fast. My prayer is this will be the start of a lifestyle of fasting for you.

3) **Ask God for whom or what you are fasting.** It could be yourself, your family, your church, your ministry, your pastor, a friend, a private situation, or circumstance. It could also be a combination of multiple things. Whatever it is, ask God to reveal it to you.

PRAYER

God, I come before You right now and ask You to give me strength to fast. I deny myself before You, and ask You to reveal to me how I need to fast and for whom or what I am fasting. In the moments where I am weak and hungry, help me to turn to You and Your Word for strength. In Jesus' name, amen.

DAY 9:
ENCOURAGEMENT

"If it is encouraging, let him encourage."

Romans 12:8 (NIV)

"

AS WE LET OUR
OWN LIGHT SHINE,
WE UNCONSCIOUSLY
GIVE OTHER PEOPLE
PERMISSION TO DO
THE SAME.

— NELSON MANDELA

ENCOURAGEMENT

Justin was a special kid. He was the child every teacher at Upson Lee South Elementary hoped they would get to teach in their class. He was also the one kid every student hoped would join his or her team at recess. His smile lit up the room, and his energy was contagious. Year after year, I hoped I would walk in on the first day of school and see him sitting in my class. Even though we never had a class together, I got to know him during lunchtime and at recess out on the playground. I wanted to be around him because he was unique in more ways than one.

Justin was a special needs child with a condition caused from a reaction to a vaccination he received as an infant. Even though he needed help with many ordinary things, he still thrived in life. Looking back now, it is evident to me that God gave him the gift of encouragement. Every person who came in contact with him saw his smile and felt loved. Their day brightened up after a simple "hello" from Justin. Every time he saw me he would say, "Noah Cleeeeeeeeveland." He was so excited to see me, he acted like it had been a hundred years since our last conversation. How could I not smile and be happy when seeing him? You could hear his laugh up and down the halls. No matter what type of day I was having, Justin brought encouragement to my soul. He also loved attention, and he would dance around mimicking workout videos he watched made by Richard Simmons. I may have just dated myself. Hey, some of you watched them, too! #thestruggleisreal

One day at lunch I noticed Justin wasn't at the table where he normally sat. I didn't really think too much of it until after it happened every day for a week. I knew something had to be wrong. This was back in the late nineties, so news didn't spread like it does today. We didn't have cell phones or Internet at our disposal, and social media wasn't part of the equation. After a week or so went by, the teacher gave us the news that Justin's mom had passed away from breast cancer. Most of us didn't even know she had it, so it was a total shocker and left a damper on our entire school. She went on to say Justin would be coming back to school in a few days and reminded all of us to be sensitive to his needs and to encourage him every chance we got. My heart broke for him, and all I could think about was how to encourage him the way he had encouraged me so many times.

When I saw him for the first time after he came back to school, I could tell he was different. His smile we all loved had disappeared. His spirit was like a wounded battleship forcing itself to stay afloat. The encouragement he so often gave was long gone. I didn't hear him say my name the way I had become accustomed to him saying it or hear that loud laugh that made me smile no matter what I was doing, and my heart hurt for him. I can't imagine how he must have felt. To lose a mother at such a young age would be tough for anyone. I had yet to come to know Christ at this time, but something inside of me wanted to change all of this. I wanted to help him. I wanted to figure out a way to bring his joy back. So I came up with a plan.

Every day at lunch and recess, I started encouraging Justin and making him laugh any way I could. I had my friends do the same. We even got him to show us one of his classic Richard Simmons workout moves. Day after day we made it a point to find him and attempt to lift his spirits. Even though there was no way for us to change the past, we could affect the present, which might benefit him in the future. Slowly but surely, I started seeing glimpses of the old Justin. A few weeks went by, and now that kid who popped in and out of every classroom on our hall, making everyone laugh, was back at it. He would see me coming from a mile away and yell my name as loud as he could: "Noah Cleeeeeeeeeveland."

The relationship I had with Justin strengthened and continued all the way through middle and high school as I started helping in his special needs class. Every day when I would get finished with my schoolwork, I would go spend time with him, helping him with his schoolwork. I spent time with him and the other kids in his classroom just loving and encouraging them. I took my guitar into their room and sang songs and laughed with them for hours. I went on field trips and other outings with them all the way until I graduated. Justin, along with some of the other kids, would only listen and respond to me, and I have to believe it stemmed from the encouragement that I gave.

One of the coolest moments of my life was walking across the graduation stage with Justin right beside me. A relationship that started from his encouragement before we were even teenagers continued as we both grew into adults. To this day, I can still find him in our hometown at a restaurant his dad started in honor of him called "Justin's Place."

Encouragement is something we all need from time to time. It keeps us going and can oftentimes confirm that we are on the right track. Have you ever heard a flock of geese fly over you and honk? I've often wondered why they fly in a V-formation.

CHURCH WITH NO WALLS: A 21-DAY CHALLENGE

Researchers have discovered that geese fly seventy-three percent farther when they fly together rather than alone. Geese use the wind created by the one in front of them, which makes flapping their wings easier. By contrast, the lead goose is taking the brunt of the headwind. In fact, the wind is so strong that if he were to look back, his neck would snap. So the reason geese honk as they fly is that they are telling the lead goose they are still behind him, staying in formation. With their encouragement, he is able to keep moving forward and doesn't have to look back. Many times, we have people "flying" with us who need to hear that we are still with them, which will support them as they move forward as well.

I wrote a song on the *Church With No Walls* album called "Miracle." The chorus starts off by saying, "The way You lift me up is a miracle." One of the greatest miracles in my life to me is how God lifts my spirits up when I'm down. And in those moments, the Holy Spirit often sends people alongside me to "honk," which brings encouragement to my soul and helps me persevere. I know you have probably been encouraged when you needed it the most, so why not ask God to use you to do the same for someone else?

While we love to be encouraged, it can be harder to be the one doing the encouraging. I know for me, the busier I get with my own issues, the less concerned I am about other people's circumstances or feelings. Romans 12 tells us that some people have the gift of encouragement, and I believe we have to become aware of its power and use it. Being compassionate toward others around us and sensitive to what they are going through can draw it out of us, just as it came out of me when I was just an elementary school kid. When people seem to have it all together, many times it's a front covering up pain. There's never a bad time to be an encourager, so let's start today!

A WORD FROM THE CHURCH...
By Tracie Gann, Business Owner

As a business owner, I come across people from all walks of life. We have a saying on our front door as you leave that says, "Be more kind than necessary, because everyone you meet is fighting some kind of battle." These are great words to live by, in my book. I try to be sensitive to the countenance of each customer by making small talk, and many times, that uncovers deeper issues. I try and always be prepared to stop and pray for anyone who needs it. To date, no one has turned down when I ask, "Can I pray for you?" There's power when we encourage those with whom we come in contact. It doesn't cost a thing to encourage, and it's priceless to those who receive it. Let your encouragement be contagious.

TODAY'S CHALLENGE

There have probably been many times you have been down and out, and God used someone to encourage you. Be compassionate today toward the people you encounter, because you never know what they are going through.

1) **Read John 4:1-42.** Notice how Jesus was not even supposed to be talking with this woman, because Jews did not associate with Samaritans. Jesus went out of His way to encourage a woman who was dealing with a lot of failure and heartache. His encouragement wound up leading many of her fellow Samaritans to believing in Him as the Messiah.

2) **Find three people to encourage today!**

PRAYER

Lord, thank You for your encouragement in my life. You have lifted me up when I was very low. I looked to the hills asking where my help comes from and found it only comes from You. Now I ask that You send the right people to me today so I can encourage them. Give me the right words to say and a prayer to pray for them. In Jesus' name, amen.

DAY 10:

FORGIVENESS

"Friend, your sins are forgiven."

Luke 5:20 (NIV)

"

FORGIVE OTHERS
NOT BECAUSE
THEY DESERVE
FORGIVENESS,
BUT BECAUSE YOU
DESERVE PEACE.

— JONATHAN
   LOCKWOOD HUIE

DAY 10:

FORGIVENESS

Growing up, I listened to a lot of hip-hop and rap music. It was before Lecrae and Christian rap broke onto the scene. I've heard many people complain about most of today's Christian music all sounding the same, but boy, this sure seemed true in most of the rap songs I grew up listening to back then. It all had the same message of drugs, abuse, sex, alcohol, war, weapons, and revenge. The stories usually started with someone killing a family member; and then, ten years down the road, eight people were left dead, and the war of revenge continued. In the hip-hop culture, it was a vicious cycle that just continued with no resolve. What if, at some point, one side decided to forgive the other? Calling a truce would not have sold as many records, but the war would have probably stopped. The problem is forgiveness goes against every part of our being.

In a fight, people tend to emulate their opponent. The more aggressive one side becomes, the harder the other side usually responds. In fact, many times the one who is retaliating comes back fighting even more aggressively. The Old Testament actually teaches "an eye for an eye, a tooth for a tooth" (Exodus 21:24). It's called *lex talionis*, which means "the law of retaliation." This mindset is whatever you do to me, I can do the same to you. In the

Old Testament, this was a system put in place to maintain justice in society. It was a way to stop crime. As a matter of fact, some cultures in the world today actually still practice this method. The issue with humans and retaliation is how it escalates the situation. Retaliation is usually motivated by anger and generally fights back harder than the original offense. It causes a person to be filled with revenge. Therefore, it hits back harder than it was hit. It steals more than was stolen. It kills more than was killed. However, many would argue God's intention for lex talionis was grace. He is very aware of our hearts and how revenge can grow inside of us when we are offended. Taking an eye for an eye was actually more difficult, because the sinful man would rather take both eyes.

When my wife and I have disagreements, the moment usually escalates as long as aggressiveness is shown from both sides. But all it takes is one of us to back down or show grace, and the other usually backs off their attack as well. Even if we both feel wronged, we are able to get it worked out. Working it out usually looks like one of us asking for forgiveness, with the other

"It's the hardest thing to give away And the last thing on your mind today

It always goes to those that don't deserve

It's the opposite of how you feel

When the pain they caused is just too real

It takes everything you have just to say the word

Forgiveness"

Matthew West
"Forgiveness"

following suit. Saying "I'm sorry" can be very powerful. Showing grace can be even more powerful. Jesus taught His disciples about forgiveness when He prayed, "Forgive us our debts, as we also have forgiven our debtors" (Matthew 6:12, ESV). Paul echoed this teaching telling us we are to forgive one another as Christ has forgiven us (Ephesians 4:32; Colossians 3:13). When someone feels wronged, the sinful nature of our inner man urges us to lash out in attack mode. We become like battleships in a war fighting with words. At the same time, when one side waves the white flag, the war usually stops.

One of the greatest moments of surrender in war history came in the Battle at Ulm. On October 20, 1805, French emperor Napoleon cornered the bulk of the Austrian army after a five-day battle in Bavaria. After being surrounded with no chance of escape, Austrian General Mack waved the white flag, giving Napoleon almost sixty thousand prisoners with minimal casualties on both sides. Legend has it that Mack attempted to surrender his sword to Napoleon at the surrender ceremony, only for the French emperor to allow him to keep it.

It's very hard to continue attacking when someone has laid down his or her weapons. But isn't that the beauty of forgiveness? When we truly forgive someone, we disarm them of their weaponry and battle plans.

Jesus paid the ultimate price for you and me when He surrendered His life, even though we didn't deserve it. He was arrested, beaten, tried, and crucified for something He never did. There are not many things in life worse than being accused of something you know you didn't do. Take it one step further, and think about being arrested and sentenced for that crime.

Growing up with a sister who was a few years older than me resulted in many wars at 152 Denham Road in Thomaston,

Georgia. It seemed like we lived on a battlefield in the midst of a continuous *Braveheart* movie. The goal in our young lives was to take the other out by getting them in trouble. After school was over, we readied ourselves for battle. One instance that always sticks out to me was a day that will live in infamy...just kidding. My sister Tasha had her boyfriend come over when my parents were not home. Of course, she told me not to tell anyone he was there. How many times had I heard, "Don't tell Mama and Daddy" before? While in the kitchen making a sandwich that day, her boyfriend knocked my mom's favorite flower vase off the counter, and it shattered into a thousand pieces on the floor. We all knew my mama was going to flip out, and my daddy would turn into the Incredible Hulk. That was when Tasha said the famous words... again, "We can't tell Mama or Daddy. If they find out, we are dead." I looked at her and, in the most serious voice I could muster, I said, "WE? You are dead, not me. And when you're gone, I'm moving into your room."

As my sister picked up the pieces of the vase, she and her boyfriend began to devise a plan to get them out of the mess they had created. There was only one problem; her snotty-nosed brat of a brother saw the whole thing. When you have a sibling growing up, knowing a secret about their dirty laundry is worth more than gold. So, they offered me a pretty sweet deal including some baseball cards and a video game as long as I didn't snitch. Could I really turn down some of my favorite players' rookie cards and Super Mario Kart? This turn of events seemed to be working out in my favor, or so I thought. One thing none of us thought about in all the wheeling and dealing was what happens when Mom realizes the vase is missing? I guess we just thought sweeping it up and throwing it in the neighbor's garbage can would solve the problem. "Maybe she'd forget about it," we thought. When you are young and dumb, you usually miss a crucial piece of evidence.

Later that evening my parents came home from work, and it was business as usual for everybody. I played in my room while my sister was in hers. Dinnertime was a little nerve-racking, as Tasha and I made eye contact a few times knowing what the other was thinking; but everyone kept their cool. Her silence meant not being on restriction for the rest of her life and becoming a nun, while mine meant baseball and Nintendo. Before we knew it, we were off to school again the next morning and back to normal. As a kid, it always felt like if you could just make it through the night and into the next day, any trouble you were in would magically disappear. Boy did I learn that this was only a myth.

The next day I remember thinking, *I can't believe we pulled it off! This had to have been one of the greatest cover-ups in the history of broken flower vases.* They say most things are "too good to be true!" Well, there's some great wisdom in that statement. That evening when my mom came home, things took a turn for the worse. I heard her call for my sister to come into the kitchen, and they talked for a few minutes. I tried to listen from the crack underneath my door, but all I could hear was mumbling. Then I heard the loud words, "Noah Stephen Cleveland." The only time my mom called me by my full name was when I was in trouble. I knew immediately we were busted but tried to walk in the room confidently portraying that I wasn't a part of such a heinous crime. I was just an innocent bystander, which in some ways was true. As I walked into the kitchen, my mom said, "Son, why were you playing with the football in the house? I've told you things will get broken. Now my vase is destroyed."

I looked at my sister who wore an evil grin, and said *"WHAT?"* At that exact moment my dad walked through the door with his usual impeccable timing that he always seemed to have when I was doing something stupid. Things began to spiral out of control when he got involved. My dad's motto was the more we talked, the worse it would be on us. After a few minutes of uncomfortable questions and silence, Tasha was sent to her room followed by moans that spread through the house. The interrogation continued with me, followed by a belt to my rear end as well. I tried to plead my case but was still put on restriction and sent to my room, and this meant no video games. There was no defending my side of the story. I was wrongfully accused. *How could my sister do this?* I thought. Bitterness rose up inside of me, and I was angry. For days I was furious at her. I held my end of the deal up by not snitching, and then of all things, I was thrown under the bus for something I didn't even do. She was the one in the wrong, but I got the short end of the stick. What made matters worse was I never received the baseball cards or video game I was promised, because not long after the incident, my sister and her boyfriend broke up.

I'm sure we've all been wronged in our lives. I would imagine you have stories just like this involving siblings, friends, parents, children, co-workers, or even spouses. Some incidents may be very painful and may have even resulted in a traumatic event in your life. We hold a grudge when we become angry and bitter because it feels like the right thing to do. Most of the time it just feels natural. The problem is, the person in bondage over the matter is you. Just like my sister, who probably doesn't even remember the incident even happened, quickly moved on with her life. The person stuck in a cage because of what took place was me. I was the one who needed to be set free, not her. Holding onto a grudge will eat at you for as long as you have it in your possession. You wait and wait for the other person to make it right, just like I did; but the truth is, they may never make it right. Sometimes we are bitter about a situation, and the person involved doesn't even realize they wronged us. At that point, we're holding onto anger that will never be resolved until it's laid down. When we forgive, the prisoner we truly set free is ourself.

Jesus showed us this example when He was on the cross. Here's a man who was wrongly accused and sentenced to death. If anyone ever deserved to hold a grudge, it was Jesus. But as the guilty mocked an innocent man, He showed the way for all of us to follow in Luke 23:34, ESV: "Jesus said, Father forgive them, for they know not what they do."

A WORD FROM THE CHURCH...
By Tara Mendias, Business Owner

It's not easy forgiving someone who has hurt you. Unforgiveness is a bondage no one should live in. It destroys you from the inside out. When you choose not to forgive, bitterness gets lodged in your heart and begins a dangerous journey that will eventually poison every area of your life if it's not squashed out. But what about those people who hurt you; you forgive them, and then they hurt you again and again and again? That's where I turn to the Scripture found in Mathew 18:21-22, NIV "Then came Peter to Jesus, and asked, 'Lord, how many times shall I forgive my brother or sister who sins against me? Up to seven times?' Jesus answered, 'I tell you not seven times, but seventy-seven times.'"

My mother is that person in my life. It took me a long time to forgive her for things that happened in my childhood. Then as an adult, I took even more devastating blows from her. That's when the words of Jesus became real to me. It wasn't easy, and I didn't want to forgive again. If I forgave her again, it would leave me vulnerable to being hurt...again!

No one wants to experience that kind of pain over and over. So what do we do? We talk about it with our friends. We think about it constantly. We water the seed of bitterness that's planted in us until it grows into an ugly monster that has taken over our lives. We can't live that way. We can't do it alone, and Jesus is the only way. His strength allows us to understand and achieve true forgiveness. Without forgiveness, we're doomed to a life lacking true JOY.

I've learned through these difficult times that forgiveness is more for me than it is for my mom. Forgiveness has released her, but it has also set me free!

TODAY'S CHALLENGE

Forgiveness takes a lot of courage and forces us to swallow our pride. Sometimes we can block out the times we were wronged, bury them deep inside of us, and think they're gone. The issue with this method is the hurt remains with us until we deal with it. You may have moved on, but have you really forgiven? Could we actually be holding onto a grudge against someone when God has forgiven us for the same thing or something very similar? We forgive because we have been forgiven. Let's be a forgiven forgiver!

1) **Read Luke 6:27-36.**

2) **Through prayer, find people you need to forgive, or ask for forgiveness.** Allow the Holy Spirit to reveal to you the depths of your soul and things that you may have buried deep inside because of something someone may have did or said to you.

3) **Search your heart today, and see if you need to forgive yourself for something you've done in the past.** Many times the enemy wants us to hold onto our past actions or mistakes when God has already forgiven them. It may be time for you to forgive yourself for things that should no longer hold you captive.

PRAYER

God, thank You for Your forgiveness. I am not worthy of it, but by Your grace, I have been saved. Your grace and love is sufficient for me, and I want to show it to others. Help me let go of times in my life where I have been wronged. It was painful, but it's time for me to find freedom. I ask that You help me with the bitterness and anger I may have toward someone who has wronged me. You loved me when I was unlovable, and I need You to help me show that same love today. In Jesus' name, amen.

DAY 11:
REST

"Come away by yourselves to a desolate place and rest for a while."

Mark 6:31 (ESV)

"

LIFE MOVES PRETTY
FAST. IF YOU DON'T
STOP AND LOOK
AROUND ONCE IN A
WHILE, YOU COULD
MISS IT.

— FERRIS BUELLER

DAY 11:

REST

Have you ever stopped to think about how far we've come as a human race with science and technology? I am only thirty-one years old, but things have changed drastically in my lifetime. I can still remember playing with a Lite Brite and watching movies on a VCR. Many of you can remember toys and devices much older than those. Now we live in an age of iPads and Blu-ray players. We even have phones that allow us to pay for an order at a register, communicate with anyone around the world in mere seconds, and take high quality pictures and video.

The progress we've seen is really astonishing, but has it in some ways become a detour? Progress in life is what we are all living for, in a sense. Taking that next step in college, then in marriage, then in our careers, then with our children. Then we help them repeat the same process, but hopefully, much quicker and more efficiently. The world we live in is busier than it's ever been as we all continue to advance in our own ways. On the surface it seems the only way to keep moving forward is to channel our inner Energizer Bunny. We have to go, go, go, and then go some more. If we stop, then we will surely get passed by and lose what we've been chasing after so hard. That's at least the natural way of thinking by many, and even if we aren't thinking about it, our habits drive us toward it.

So the question is, when do we stop? When do we take a break to rest? Surely we all get tired, right? Fifteen years ago the average person worked five days a week, but today, the average is six days a week. That model allows one day for rest. For some of us one day may be enough, but for most, it's not. The problem is, no matter how many "days off" we technically have from our jobs, they are not used for rest. Usually, we cram other things into those days to the point they too feel like shifts at work. We have things like sporting events for our kids to attend, four-hour grocery runs, and the remodeling project that's been going on for three years. As humans we have limits, and so do the people around us. When we push past our limits, something has to give. That something is usually our sanity and the sanity of the people around us. Every decision we make affects those closest to us. As a leader of my family and ministry, I have to think about the ripple effect my decisions will have on my family. My relationships will indeed suffer when they are put on the back burner. The reality is, we often push ourselves past our breaking points without even knowing it. Oftentimes when this occurs, it's too late, as the damage can be too severe to be fixed. This can lead to divorce, loss of job, debt, drugs, alcohol, jail time, and even suicide. Operating outside our limits can be a very dangerous thing.

> As humans we have limits, and so do the people around us.

So how can we avoid these dangers? There are numerous approaches we could take for how to avoid these things, but one simple way I have found is to rest. God commanded the Israelites in Exodus 20 to "Remember the Sabbath day by keeping it holy. Six days you shall labor and do all your work, but the seventh day is a Sabbath to the Lord your God. On it you shall not do any work." The definition of the word *Sabbath* in the *New Oxford American Dictionary* is:

> *"A day of religious observances and abstinence from work, kept by Jews from Friday evening to Saturday evening, and by most Christians on Sunday."*

I know I have failed to keep the Sabbath holy in my life for many years. As a minister, my job requires me to be in work mode most Sundays out of the year. By the time Monday hits, I'm covered up with traveling, responding to emails, phone calls, and meetings. I repeat this process again until the next weekend rolls around when it's usually time to go to another city to sing or preach. So where does my rest come into play? Where does the time I spend with my family start? I struggle with the same addiction that twenty-five percent of Americans do—overworking.

For a long time, my wife continued to ask me to take a day off and just be with her and our boys, but it was not until I pushed past my limits that I actually listened. Sure, I would take days here and there, but I never placed any boundaries to keep me accountable and fresh. Being burnt out is something we don't even realize can happen. As a matter of fact, most of us are burnt out well before we even realize it has happened. People around us see the signs way before we see them ourselves, as we are so focused on progress and our next step in life.

One of my favorite songs I have ever written is called "Until Only You Remain." The first line says, *"When silence is the only sound."* In a fast-paced world, being silent doesn't really seem like an option. But over and over we see Jesus going into a time of solitude and silence. He tells His disciples to do this very thing on more than one occasion. In the crucible of ministry, at the time when their lives were the busiest, He would lead them into a place to be alone. In Mark 6:31, ESV He said, "Come away by yourselves to a desolate place and rest for a while." This was at a time when Jesus had just sent them out in power to preach, to heal, and to cast out demons. So I find it very interesting how immediately following this, He led them into a time of rest.

I believe if we're honest with ourselves, there are many seasons in life where we have little to no margin. Coming to grips with this was key for me in my life to remain the disciple, husband, father, and leader I am called to be for my family and ministry. After experiencing burn-out, I knew I had to implement some boundaries that would allow me to rest properly. We may think we are super-human and can do everything at one time, but it's just not possible. I know that's what I thought, but reality came crashing down on top of me, and it not only affected my life, but also those closest to me.

A few weeks ago, my wife and I took our youngest son, Zeek, to his doctor to check out a problem with his soft spot bulging out on top of his head. We quickly saw his doctor had pushed himself way beyond his limits. The moment he came in the room he was frazzled. He couldn't concentrate and kept complaining about everyone in the office. He complained about his patients and could barely even type on his computer or communicate his thoughts. He was having such a hard time focusing, he was not able to diagnose Zeek with anything, and he basically just read information from the Internet like he had no medical degree or expertise at all. I'm sure if he was operating inside margins and had proper rest, he would have had no problem figuring out the proper diagnosis. However, his lack of focus hindered him from using his gifts properly and led us to search for a new doctor. This experience also made me wonder how many times that happens to us, as well, in our own lives.

There is no question that the hardest regimen in my life is to rest and take time off. It takes great faith and discipline for me to stop, knowing the fast-paced world is still working around me. Creating margins and limits in our life will help us all in a tremendous way, as long as we abide in them and honor their boundaries. Doing so will actually make us more effective and productive and will help our progress in the long run.

A WORD FROM THE CHURCH...
By Kacie Hoard, Stay-at-home Mother

Rest, what rest? It's hard to rest being a stay-at-home mom. After telling my grandmother I had been up with my sick two-year-old all through the night, she responded by saying, "A father's job lasts sunrise to sunset, but a mother's job lasts all day and all night." She's right. It never stops. There is always something to be done and someone who needs me. It can be a vicious cycle and can leave me weary and tired. With all the demands of being a stay-at-home mom, rest isn't on the agenda. We get so busy taking care of our entire family that our time with God and ourselves is put on the back burner. Many times we even feel guilty setting aside time to rest because it only feels natural to care for others' needs first.

We get our to-do list out and check off all the tasks that have been completed, never noticing that our name is all the way at the bottom or not even on our list at all. Moms, this is how we end up completely drained, overwhelmed, and exhausted. If we can't take care of ourselves physically, emotionally, and spiritually, there is no way we can be the wife or mom that God has called us to be.

Morning quiet times can be impossible in my home. If I wake up extra early and sit down with my coffee and Bible, inevitably one of my children awakens. We only have small windows of time. Even if it's five minutes, we must give it to God. We can talk to Him when we're feeding our baby, while in the shower, or while folding laundry. We can even turn on the Bible app while cooking breakfast. We must take the time to remember what He has done for us and thank Him for it. If we're too busy striving, we'll miss the blessing.

TODAY'S CHALLENGE

In the middle of a busy world, rest is something that will help you as you move forward and continue this journey of being a *church with no walls*. You are called by God, just like the disciples were; and Jesus commanded them to rest, so it's time for you to do the same.

1) **Read Mark 4:35-41.** Notice even in the middle of a HUGE storm, Jesus was resting. He was actually asleep on a cushion.

2) **Use today as a day of rest.** You may still have to go to school or work, but be sensitive to moments throughout the day where you would normally be crazy busy, and replace those moments with solitude. Instead of hanging out with friends at lunch, find a spot to be alone and rest. Instead of listening to music, just relax in silence. When you get home, find a time and place to relax and rest.

3) **Take today and assess your lifestyle.** Where are you pushing past your limits? Write these areas down and monitor them closely.

4) **Take the things you've written down and ask God to show you how you can place boundaries in your life in order to stay within your limits.**

PRAYER

God, I ask right now that You reveal to me where I am pushing past my human limits. Help me implement margins in my daily life. Give me a conviction for keeping the Sabbath day holy, even in a busy world. In Jesus' name, amen.

DAY 12:
OUTREACH

"You give them something to eat..."

Mark 6:37 (ESV)

"

DARE TO REACH
OUT YOUR HAND
INTO THE
DARKNESS, TO PULL
ANOTHER HAND
INTO THE LIGHT.

— NORMAN B. RICE

OUTREACH

Right after Jesus went into a time of solitude (Matthew 14:13), we see the story of one of the greatest miracles ever recorded in the Bible. Jesus, along with his disciples, fed five thousand men, not counting the women and children. To think about what occurred is truly amazing. Jesus took fives loaves of bread and two fish, and fed ALL those people. There was even food left over. The lessons Jesus taught His disciples were ongoing, but we see in this instance the power of outreach. You've probably heard the word "outreach" thrown around in your church by your pastor or one of the staff members, but have you ever been a part of it? Have you ever considered maybe God wants you to have a heart for outreach?

Outreach is a perfect picture of what being a *church with no walls* is all about. Moving our faith from inside the building to the outside world requires a great deal of effort on our part. It requires a selfless attitude and a servant's heart. In a moment of action, we put all our needs behind someone else's and serve them whole-heartedly. Many churches go into their communities to help people from all walks of life who represent many different needs. Through our ministry, we get a chance to travel and experience a lot of churches, all of which have different methods and cultures. One thing I have noticed while traveling is the churches who are growing or have already grown in number are led by pastors and a team who spend a great deal of time and resources reaching outside the walls of their building.

Outreach can wear different hats. You may have gone on a mission trip, served food to needy people, given out toys at Christmas to children who otherwise would go without, helped when a natural disaster occurred, and even dropped some change into a bucket when someone was ringing a bell at the front door of a local store. No matter what types of outreach we have been a part of, we have to allow it to be a part of our everyday life.

The world is full of people who are hurting. It may be hard for us to fathom poverty, hunger, homelessness, or unemployment unless we've walked in someone else's shoes. But are we really supposed to fathom it? Are we meant to always understand why someone is in the predicament they are in? Are we supposed to judge them because they are solely responsible for their circumstance? No way! Maybe we are never meant to know a person's situation when they stand in front of us with great need. It's easy to ask for proof that they are worthy of our help before we actually reach out our hand, but Jesus showed us otherwise when He simply loved people with no questions asked.

> "One of the subtlest burdens God ever puts on us as saints is the burden of discernment concerning other souls."
>
> **Oswald Chambers**
> Author of
> *My Utmost For His Highest*

One trait that will help us with a heart of outreach is compassion. Over and over in the

Gospels, we read where Jesus was moved with compassion when He served. Having compassion will move us, as well, to reach out to people who need it most. Having compassion is a deep emotion that moves us in our core being and allows us to look past the cause of the situation and be a part of the solution. It also moves us to action. Many of the stories we may encounter in life will be filled with people who are struggling with the very things that we once struggled with, and the only difference between us is we overcame the struggle or situation. We have to ask ourselves this question: How did we overcome it? Have you ever thought that maybe God used someone in the midst of your struggles to reach out to you? That was a form of outreach. That person was moved by compassion when they helped you. What if that person had asked you a series of questions before extending a helping hand? I know I'm glad someone loved me beyond my obvious circumstances. You may have never experienced an extreme case of need like some, but it doesn't mean you weren't worth someone's outreach.

In the previous challenge we talked about how we as humans are so busy we have little time for anything or anyone else, so we have to be even more alert and aware of people who may need a helping hand. I know I have been so busy at times in my life that I've missed opportunities from the Lord to reach out to someone in great need. Being aware of our surroundings will help us see where outreach is needed. It may lead us to those organized outreach events, but it very well may be a still small voice when we are running wide open on a busy afternoon in our everyday life. In my experience, it has been a little bit of both. I have to be ready and willing for outreach at all times in my life, because after all, wasn't Jesus?

A WORD FROM THE CHURCH...

By Darryl Bellar, Lead Pastor at Journey Church in Fernandina Beach, Florida

As the lead pastor of three different locations and having had the privilege of coaching other pastors, I've discovered most churches fall into two categories: a congregation-minded church or a community-minded church. The difference is rather simple. One is a church with no walls that grows by transformation, and the other is a church that mostly grows by transfer. The Bible says in Acts 1:8, "You will receive power when the Holy Spirit comes on you; and you shall be witnesses to Me in Jerusalem, and in all Judea and Samaria, and to the ends of the earth."

We are the Church, and Jesus commanded us to GO. In fact, He said this in Matthew 25:42-45: "'For I was hungry, and you didn't feed Me. I was thirsty, and you didn't give Me a drink. I was a stranger, and you didn't invite Me into your home. I was naked, and you didn't give Me clothing. I was sick and in prison, and you didn't visit Me.' Then they will reply, 'Lord, when did we ever see You hungry or thirsty or a stranger or naked or sick or in prison, and not help You?' And He will answer, 'I tell you the truth, when you refused to help the least of these, my brothers and sisters, you were refusing to help Me.'"

TODAY'S CHALLENGE

When looking at the life of our Savior, we see He was the solution everywhere He went. If we claim to be a follower of Jesus, then "we must walk as He did" (1 John 2:6). There's no way for us to claim to be a Christian if we don't make outreach a part of our everyday life.

1) **Read Matthew 25:35-40.**

2) **Look for someone who is in need of help or in an unfortunate situation, and reach out to him or her.** Pray that God will lead you to the right person and that you will help them in the right way.

3) **Find out what type of outreach program your church has or is a part of, and sign up to serve at their next event.**

PRAYER

God, I ask You to place inside of me compassion. Let my heart not be hardened, but moved, just like Jesus was moved. I want to be a part of the solution. Let outreach become part of my DNA and lifestyle. In Jesus' name, amen.

DAY 13:

FEARLESS

"For God gave us a spirit not of fear, but of power and love and self-control."

2 Timothy 1:7 (ESV)

"

BEING FEARLESS
IS HAVING A LOT OF
FEARS, BUT YOU
JUMP ANYWAY.

— TAYLOR SWIFT

DAY 13:

FEARLESS

I've shared a lot about my wife, Ivy, so I think it's time for you to hear from her. She inspires me every day to be a better Christ follower, husband, father, and leader. Her persistence and fearlessness is contagious. I felt it was only fitting for her to write this challenge.

The word *fear* is mentioned 365 times in the Bible, which is the exact number of days in a year. Could the amount of times fear is mentioned have anything to do with the fact our Father in heaven knew this one thing would become so dominant in the lives of His people that we would need one promise for every day? I would answer with a big ole (like we say in the south) YEAH! Throughout your life I'm sure you've experienced fear in some shape, form, or fashion; because we all have. I, for one, struggle with worry and anxiety, along with tons of other emotions that go along with being fearful. So today I would like to share with you my story and how God helped me face my fears head on and be victorious.

Just to give you a little background on me... I longed to be a mom from the time I was a little girl. Growing up playing house in my room, I hung out with an imaginary family, carried around baby dolls, cooked in a toy kitchen, and had just about anything a little girl could get her hands on to make her feel like a mommy. I just knew I was destined to be a mother to many children. As I got older, I loved talking with friends and hearing about the big dreams and expectations they had for their lives—things like going to college, getting married, and starting careers were at the top of all their lists. Even though I knew all those things were in my future, my dream burned inside of me and remained the same from my childhood days. There was nothing in this world I wanted more than to be a mom.

Noah and I were high school sweethearts. We grew up together, so we've shared many memories. We've been together now fifteen years. I still remember us talking about what our family would look like while we were still freshmen in high school. Yes, it was a bit early, but we always felt we were meant to be together. After college, we got married. I went to cosmetology school and became a hairdresser and loved it. Noah had just started getting his music career off the ground, so we were living the dream, right? I loved our time together with just the two of us, but deep down, I still longed for that day when I would hear a baby crying, bathwater running, and little gibberish that sounded like "mommy" for the first time. Walking through stores and looking at baby outfits was my idea of shopping. After four years of marriage, Noah mentioned casually one day that he felt it was time for us to start a family. *What? Are you serious?* I thought. Finally, everything I had dreamed of was about to become reality. I was on cloud nine, praising the Lord with every ounce of my being. This was the moment I had waited for my entire life.

Then one night, only a few weeks later, I had a dream. In my dream I was shopping at Dollar Tree (this girl loves some Dollar Tree) on aisle five, and I saw the devil standing in front of me. He was dressed as a woman; although, it was the ugliest, scariest, and most hateful looking woman I had ever seen. She looked at me, pointed to my stomach, and said, "You will never conceive a child, and even if you do, you will never have that child, because it will die." I immediately woke up in a complete panic. I remember being so afraid. Full of fear, I went to work the next day trying to muster up enough courage to forget what I saw in my dream. I knew if I could just laugh and enjoy spending time with my clients, I'd be fine.

If you're a woman, you know the reason you go to a salon is to tell your life story. You want to laugh, cry, and of course, you want to come out with the most beautiful hair, feeling good about yourself. Hearing stories and encouraging my clients was what I loved most about my job. On this particular day, though, hearing their stories made my fears worse. Two of my clients that day shared very tragic stories. The first woman told me how she had tried to conceive a child for over seven years but could not do so no matter how much they tried. She went on to tell me how she was broken and left with many questions. I confidently told her that God would be her strength, and not to give up, even though internally I was a mess. I also shared with her what Galatians 6:9 says: "And let us not grow weary of doing good, for in due season we will reap a harvest, if we do not give up."

I greeted the second client and asked how she was doing, and with a broken spirit she said, "Not good." She began to tell me a similar story about how she had tried for years to get pregnant, but couldn't. And when it finally happened, she had to deliver the baby prematurely. Her experience of holding her little girl for only two hours before she passed away from complications left me shaken and afraid.

At this point it was getting real. I went into our break room as the woman's hair processed under the dryer with color and started to cry. I cried because I just knew this was the Lord preparing me to not be able to conceive a child. To make matters worse, this happened six more times with new clients over the next few weeks, as they all had similar stories. I was so overwhelmed with fear that I felt I couldn't even breathe. It was like I was trapped in a room with no way out. You see, I had allowed the enemy to convince me this was God's will and that He was preparing me to go through something horrible. My faith had become crippled, but it was all a lie.

One night in the midst of this season, I had yet another dream, except this time it was God speaking to me. I did not see Him, but I heard His voice. He said, "Ivy! You will conceive a son, and you will name him Samuel. And just as Samuel was in the Bible, so your Samuel will be." When I woke up, I immediately wrote everything God had told me down in my journal. All the fear, which had previously filled my life, immediately disappeared when the Lord spoke to me. He replaced my fear with faith. I knew now because my Father had said it, there was no doubt it was going to happen. I also learned an important lesson through all of this. God is not the author of confusion or fear, but of peace and clarity. I am so glad that God's words are powerful enough to offset anything the enemy says to us.

After only three months of trying to get pregnant, I conceived a child. My hopes and dreams were finally becoming my reality, and the greatest gift behind my salvation and husband was on its way. To find out later we were having a boy humbled me and brought so much joy, because I knew that the God of all creation had spoken to me about this. He gave me a promise that I get to hold in my arms every day. And I get to call him "Samuel," a name given to him by our Father in heaven.

Of course, fear still tries to creep into my life, but allowing God to speak His Word over me instead of listening to the enemy is pivotal for me to overcome it. I believe when we let God have the say in the midst of our fear, we will see our faith come to life. Everyone deals with fear, but the weapon we use to fight it will make all the difference. Choose today to listen to the Voice of Truth in the midst of your fears.

A WORD FROM THE CHURCH...
By Noel Miller, Missionary to Brussels, Belgium

Being a new missionary, I often think about moving away from everything I know. It is what I want to give my life to, but I still let one thing set in at times...fear. My husband, two boys, and I are saying yes to a journey with Jesus to work with Convoy of Hope in Brussels, Belgium. When I took a trip there, I got off the train to a city covered with armed guards. Many of the recent terrorist attacks in Europe were planned in Brussels, and a few were actually executed there. BBC News stated that, outside of the Middle East, Belgium has the most "home grown" jihadists being trained for terrorism. We are just a few months away from moving our family there. Our boys are two and five. The easy thing to do would be to let fear win and play it safe.

There is a story in the Bible you are probably familiar with where Jesus was in a boat with His disciples, and the storms began to rage. The disciples thought they were about to die and began to anxiously try to wake Jesus. He woke up and calmly used His voice to bring the storms to a halt. Jesus was peacefully asleep during a storm that gripped them with fear.

When you fast forward through the Gospels you come to another story where the roles are reversed. It takes place in the Garden of Gethsemane.

Jesus is now awake, and the disciples are sleeping. He urges them to stay awake and describes it as a crucial time to pray, but still they slept. They could not stay awake for what was truly important.

Note this: Jesus is asleep to fear but awake to the dreams that are in your heart to accomplish what He has for you. I pray that you are encouraged today knowing "playing it safe" is not the answer. His perfect love drives out what keeps us from doing what we are meant to do. It is time to step out into the storm and walk on water.

TODAY'S CHALLENGE

Fear doesn't always encompass things like being afraid of heights, snakes, spiders, etc., but many times, it is the small things we fixate our minds on which keep us from focusing on Jesus. Only you know what fears you need to deal with today, so I challenge you to give them to your Father who has the ability to take away fear and replace it with faith.

1) **Read Matthew 14:22-33.** Pay attention to how fear crippled Peter when he took his eyes off Jesus. In order to defeat fear and "walk on the water," we must keep our eyes fixed on Jesus, not on our circumstances or even our feelings.

2) **Write down your biggest fears, and throughout the day, find ways to face each one head on. Cross them off after you've faced them.**

3) **Find someone to share some of your fears with, and ask them to name their biggest fears.** Offer to pray for them about their fears.

PRAYER

Father, help me surrender all my fear and anxiety to You. Help me to be empowered through Your Word and not through my circumstances. You are a big God, so help me see You today as I choose to take on my fears with boldness. In Jesus' name, amen.

DAY 14:

WORDS

"For out of the abundance of the heart the mouth speaks."

Matthew 12:34 (ESV)

"

KIND WORDS
CAN BE SHORT
AND EASY
TO SPEAK, BUT
THEIR ECHOES ARE
TRULY ENDLESS.

— MOTHER TERESA

DAY 14:

WORDS

They've made me feel like a prisoner
They've made me feel set free
They've made me feel like a criminal
They've made me feel like a king
They've lifted my heart to places I've never been
They've dragged me down back to where I began

Words can build you up
Words can break you down
Start a fire in your heart or put it out

Let my words be life
Let my words be truth
I don't wanna say a word
Unless it points the world back to You

Those are the lyrics from the hit song, "Words," written by Jonathan Steingard and Matt Hammitt and performed by the Christian band Hawk Nelson. This song changed my life when I first heard it. It impacted me, not because I had felt hurt by harmful words used by others toward me, but because I have been the one spitting them out. We can get really comfortable just saying whatever we feel and never stop to think about the result that comes from the words we speak. As the lyrics state above, our words can bring life to others or do some major damage. Proverbs 18:21 says, "Death and life are in the power of the tongue." Isn't it weird how our words feel so powerless at times, though? Words are like baby snakes. While they seem harmless, they can be more poisonous than the adult snakes, because baby snakes can't control the amount of venom in their bite.

Most of us never think twice about the words we use, but maybe words are something that need to be monitored in our lives. James 3 says that our tongue "is a restless evil, full of deadly poison." Surely something like that needs to be tamed, right?

In Matthew 12:34-36 Jesus says, "For out of the abundance of the heart the mouth speaks. The good man brings good things out of the good stored up in him, and the evil man brings evil things out of the evil stored up in him." He even takes it a step further and says, "We will have to give an account on the Day of Judgment for every careless word we have spoken." So when it comes to the words we use, there is probably a backstory behind each one that we will answer for on the Day of Judgment. And according to Jesus, the things we say come from what has been stored up inside of us. It's no secret we are all sinners and have the innate ability to sin inside of us; so monitoring our words means we have to monitor what's on the inside very closely. Having the tendency to sin, we have to be careful as to what goes into our soul, because it could be a very poisonous combination. What goes in will come out.

I read a story once about a fourteen-year-old girl from Indiana named Angel. Angel had been a victim of severe bullying. The hurtful words and actions aimed at her did so much damage that she committed suicide. She purposely hanged herself from a tree in front of her bus stop, so that her tormentors would see her lifeless body swinging back and forth. Her mother found a suicide note containing the following message:

Why did I deserve this pain? Have you ever thought about what you did to me? Huh...maybe not! Because you killed me every day... You told me so much that I started believing it. And I was stupid for doing that. Every morning, day, and night I look in the mirror and cry and replay the harmful words in my head.

P.S. It's the bullying that killed me. Please get justice.

Bullying is an epidemic that has driven thousands of people just like Angel to the point of no return. This happens not only with children or students, but adults as well. Many adults still hear the words that were spoken to them when they were a child. Words like, "You'll never amount to anything." "You're too fat." "You're too slow." "Why can't you be like that person?"

STATS ON BULLYING

More than one out of every five students (20.8%) report being bullied. (National Center for Educational Statistics, 2016)

- 64% of children who were bullied did not report it; only 36% reported the bullying. (Petrosina, Guckenburg, DeVoe & Hanson, 2010)

- Nearly 75% of American adults have witnessed online harassment, with 40% seeing the brunt of that being cyber bullying. (Pew Research Center, 2014)

- One in six adults suffer some form of workplace bullying. (CBS New York, 2011)

- One million children on Facebook alone were harassed in 2011. (Consumer Reports)

- 90% of children in grades four though eight have been bullied at some point. (DoSomething.org)

- 53% of children have said something that was mean or hurtful to someone else online. (iSafe Foundation)

Remember the old saying, "Sticks and stones may break my bones, but words will never hurt me"? This is the furthest thing from the truth. Just ask anyone who has been a victim of hurtful words. While words may not drive some to the place it drove Angel, they will, however, stick with you forever. Once something is said, it can't be taken back. I still hear harmful words from people whom I haven't seen or talked to in many years. I am sure my wife or other people close to me have replayed my words—whether good or bad—over and over again as well. A single word can shift someone's mindset. Proverbs 15:1 says, "A soft answer turns away wrath, but a harsh word stirs up anger." Just like I won't forget some of the harmful words people have used toward me, I won't forget the helpful ones either. You and I have great opportunities every day to use words to build others up. We have the ability to lift them up when they're down. Imagine the impact you could have if the people around you received life from your words. I am sure you've been on both the receiving end and the giving end of poisonous words, so remember how it made you feel when talking to people you encounter.

Sometimes words can even change the course of history. David Chadwick writes in his book, *Eight Great Ways To Honor Your Wife*, a story about an elementary school teacher from Detroit, Michigan named Mrs. Beneduci. In the 1960s, many public schools faced racial tensions. Integration was an uphill battle that few chose to climb. But Mrs. Beneduci believed God created all people equal, and she welcomed the new African-American students into her classroom. One specific nine-year-old boy named Stephen Morris seldom spoke. He was not only black but also sight-impaired. So she came up with an idea to break down the walls of integration and build Stephen up in the process.

The class had a pet mouse that she hid in the trashcan before class, and in the middle of her teaching one day, she let the students know the mouse was missing, and they needed to find it immediately. Some students laughed, some screamed, and some stood in their seats. She asked Morris, who had an exceptional ability to hear, to see if he could find the mouse by listening for it. He asked his peers to be completely quiet, and he found him quickly in the trashcan. He was quite proud of himself. Then Mrs. Beneduci flooded Stephen's soul with life-giving words. She told him God had given him a gift to hear things other people could not. She concluded her encouragement by saying, "Stephen Morris, you are a wonder!" Thereafter, his classmates nicknamed him "Little Stevie Wonder."

In the following months, Stevie began to explore his hearing gift. This led him to an extraordinary musical talent. Some time later he recorded the first of many Gold records, *Fingertips, Part II*. Mrs. Beneduci is argued by many to be a world changer because of the words she used.

A WORD FROM THE CHURCH...

By Tony Wood, Songwriter of 29 #1 Songs and Co-writer of the Song "Church With No Walls"

I have experienced on so many occasions how words can be lifelines. Sometimes at a point of discouragement, someone who knows me well will remind me that God is sovereign over all. Sometimes when I'm feeling alone, they'll remind me that they love me. There have been notes from friends and family members I've saved for decades because they came with the right words at the right time. We have that power daily. We can go through life throwing out lifelines to others—words of hope, comfort, compassion, and understanding. What is the gospel if not the greatest lifeline that's ever been offered? Be mindful today if, perhaps, the Spirit might be leading you to write a note, send an email, make a call, shoot a text...or perhaps, most impactful of all, speak face to face with someone a word of truth, hope, or kindness that may well be the lifeline they are needing.

TODAY'S CHALLENGE

You can learn a lot about someone by just letting them talk. Within a few minutes, you will know what is stored up inside of them. What are people hearing when you talk? Words are so important that God had people write them down over the course of thousands of years. We now read them in the Bible. Use your words wisely today.

1) **Read James 1:19-26.**

2) **Choose to say something positive to everyone you talk to today.** My wife uses the phrase "negative fast." How about going on a negative fast today and choosing to say only good things the entire day?

3) **Ask one person close to you to keep you accountable with the words you are using.** Each week, ask them what they've heard coming from your mouth.

PRAYER

God, I ask that You forgive me for the poisonous words I've used in the past. Help me be aware of the words I use when I speak. Reveal what's stored up inside of me, and cleanse my soul of any poison. In Jesus' name, amen.

DAY 15:
FAILURE

*"And David sent and inquired about
the woman."*

2 Samuel 11:3 (ESV)

"

MY GREAT CONCERN
IS NOT WHETHER
YOU HAVE FAILED,
BUT WHETHER YOU
ARE CONTENT WITH
YOUR FAILURE.

— ABRAHAM LINCOLN

FAILURE

Being a king must be hard. I often think about the immense pressure the President of the United States must face on a daily basis. Being the leader of any group of people in general is really tough, and I guess that's why not just anyone can win the job or be successful at it. Being in the limelight has its advantages and disadvantages. You get to be the one calling the shots at the end of the game, but if you miss, everyone blames you for the loss. John C. Maxwell said it best in his book, *The 21 Irrefutable Laws of Leadership*: "Everything rises and falls on leadership." Your every move is on display, like you are a mannequin in the window of a shopping mall. Being a leader doesn't allow you to fail much, and if you do, you usually won't stay in a position of leadership for very long.

King David was a great leader and a man after God's own heart. God anointed David to be the man to lead the Israelites, and it was evident to everyone. He had many great victories during his reign, but a battle with a fierce enemy called lust would wind up causing great tragedy in his life and kingship. 2 Samuel 11 tells us David was up on the roof of his palace one day when he saw a woman named Bathsheba bathing down below. First of all, if you're a man, stay away from any woman with "Bath" in her name if she is not your wife. #justsayin! As a king, he could ask for anything with no questions asked. Power like that comes with great responsibility. If the small things in our life aren't kept in line, it can lead to failure. Not dealing with lust led to David's first failure in this story.

He sent a messenger to find out who she was, but he didn't stop there. His second failure was again sending someone to her, but this time, they were to bring her back to him. His third failure was sleeping with her. And just when you think it's over, Bathsheba sends word to him that she is pregnant with his child. She was married, so the truth about David's failure was about to be exposed just like a "Maury" episode. The entire city, along with her husband, was about to hear the words, "David, you are the father!" As hard as this episode would have been to watch when the truth was revealed, it would have been a better outcome had David learned from his failure early on.

Instead of admitting to failing, David makes yet another colossal mistake by bringing Bathsheba's husband, Uriah, off the battlefield. His plan was to have Uriah come home, get him drunk so that he would sleep with his wife, and then send him back to war. This scheme would have covered up the fact that David was the father, because after all, there were no DNA tests in that day to prove anything. So when everyone found out she was with child, there would be no questions asked, because her husband would have come home and made a special visit to her. The only problem with this plan was Uriah was an honest man. He had integrity. He wouldn't even go into his own house because he felt it was not fair to his fellow soldiers, considering they were still at war on the battlefield.

At this point in the story, there is still time for David to do the right thing, but yet, he fails miserably again; and this time it leads to death. He sends Uriah back to war with his own death warrant in hand, a warrant he never even opened because he honored King David so much. The letter commanded the general to put him on the frontline and retreat when attacked to ensure he was killed. Because of David's failure, an entire family was torn apart. Bathsheba gave birth to the baby, only to watch it die soon thereafter, as well.

To me, in this story, the biggest failure David committed was not owning up to it when he made his first mistake. Had he just failed once, which was the moment he watched her bathe from the rooftop and not turn away, things would have turned out completely different. God could have dealt with his heart privately, not involving Bathsheba or her husband. She would have never even talked to King David.

Everyone fails; it's inevitable, but what we do right after failure will turn out to be crucial down the road. If failure is something we all experience, then we must let God deal with it, use it, and teach us through it to make us better so that we don't let it happen again. We must learn from our mistakes and figure out what is causing them to happen. Insanity is doing the same thing over and over, expecting a different result. To avoid insanity, and yet another failure, we have to detect where the breakdown is occurring and fix it. Flipping this to a spiritual matter means we have to allow God to reveal the deep issues causing failure in us. We also have to be willing to allow Him to fix them before He can use them. Sometimes this process is painful and brings other people into the picture to help us, and that's okay.

> We must learn from our mistakes and figure out what is causing them to happen.

One encouraging note we can take out of this story from 2 Samuel is that even through his failure, God was with David. He remained king and had many great victories. God continued to help him in his walk. David eventually allowed God to deal with his sin and failure and served God for the rest of his days. He and Bathsheba had another child, a son named Solomon, who became the wisest man to ever live. Aren't you glad God remains with you and helps you through your failures? When we hear or read stories about someone else's failures, it helps us relate. It allows us to not feel so isolated in our own situation or circumstance. There is great power when we hear someone else's victory moment, as it lets us know there's hope for us, too. Your victory can inspire someone else to not only keep fighting but also win. Check out these stories of failure from a few names you might recognize...

After being rejected from his high school basketball team,
he ran home, locked himself in his room, and cried.
MICHAEL JORDAN
Six-time NBA Champion, Five-time NBA MVP,
Fourteen-time NBA All-star

His fiancé died; he failed in multiple businesses,
had a nervous breakdown, and was defeated in eight elections.
ABRAHAM LINCOLN
16th President of The United States

He was fired from a newspaper job for
"lacking imagination" and "having no original ideas."
WALT DISNEY
Creator of Mickey Mouse and the Disney brand,
winner of twenty-two Academy Awards

At the age of 30, he was devastated and depressed
after being fired from the company he started.
STEVE JOBS
Co-founder of Apple Inc. and Pixar Animation Studios

He wasn't able to speak until he was almost four years old, and
his teachers said he would "never amount to much."
ALBERT EINSTEIN
Theoretical Physicist and Nobel Prize Winner

A WORD FROM THE CHURCH...
By Pete Orta, Founder of In Triumph, Gospel Music Hall of Famer, GRAMMY® Award-Winning Guitarist for Petra

Failure takes the liberty to define us whenever it pleases, so if you wouldn't mind, I'd like to return the favor. This trickster loves to masquerade behind circumstance and blame, but the Bible is sure to strip its mask. For failure is nothing more than our realization of God's sovereignty—when our "free will" crumbles underneath his Lordship's footstool. These dark moments only force us to admit that we were never the "master of our fate" or the "captain of our soul"— just a mere vessel caught between two ripples of God's preordained plan.

Therefore, let this be a call to repentance. When we embrace our failures, we increase in Christ (John 3:30). The Apostle Paul commands us to delight in our weaknesses and hardships (2 Corinthians 12:10) for he preaches that Christ is strong in us. And although there is no wrong committed when our plans fall apart, the sin is found in not acknowledging how our misfortunes are always used, somehow, to glorify our King. Have joy in knowing "that for those who love God all things"—our victories and defeats—"work together for good, for those who are called according to His purpose." So for this reason, if "to die is gain," then to lose is victory.

TODAY'S CHALLENGE

The key to failure is to not let it define us. God wants to use our story of overcoming failure to encourage and inspire others to do the same.

1) **Read 2 Samuel 11-12.**

2) **Think back to the times you failed and overcame those failures.** What did you learn, and how did God use those mistakes?

3) **Share your experience of failure with one person.** Ask them if there is any area in their life where they are failing and need prayer. Pray with them and encourage them. Also, ask them how a specific failure has affected them.

4) **Ask a pastor, spiritual leader, or close friend to keep you accountable in any areas of your life where you may be failing repeatedly.** Be honest and up front with them.

5) **Tell your story of victory to people as often as you can.** Let them know the ways God has used a failure in your life for good.

PRAYER

God, I come before You and ask that You reveal to me any areas where I am failing. Give me the strength and boldness I need to deal with these areas. I also ask that You use my times of failure to not define me, but to encourage others who may be in the same situation. Give me courage to share my failures and how You've helped me overcome them. In Jesus' name, amen.

DAY 16:
UNITY

"That they may all be one."

John 17:21 (ESV)

"

WE ARE ONLY
AS STRONG
AS WE ARE UNITED,
AS WEAK
AS WE ARE DIVIDED.

— J.K. ROWLING

UNITY

I get the honor of traveling all over the country and partnering with many churches and organizations to serve alongside their vision. Many of the events I do consist of multiple churches attending in an effort to bring unity to their city. I have had the privilege of seeing my song, "Church With No Walls," be used as an anthem and catalyst for the Church at events like this over the past couple of years. It's really grown into something that is remarkable, and in many ways inspired this book. We are currently even doing a "Church With No Walls" Tour. Our vision for this tour is to do exactly what Jesus prayed in John 17: "that all of them may be one" and "be brought to complete unity." We want to see believers join together, and so far on this tour, we have seen some amazing things happen. Sometimes this even happens when one church unites within its own walls. I understand it's difficult to join across denominations because of theological differences, cultural differences, and even different approaches to ministry. Sometimes calendars even prevent churches from coming together. All these issues are legitimate, which is why it's so powerful when they actually do unify. Our vision for these events is not to dispute theology but to lift up the name of Jesus together with one voice, as one Church. People are much stronger when they are working together.

There's a great scene from the movie *Gladiator* that shows what unity can overcome. In the film, Maximus Decimus Meridius and his fellow gladiators are in a Roman Coliseum standing before the Emperor and a bloodthirsty crowd ready to face whatever enemies Caesar sends out to kill them. Maximus says to his men, "Whatever comes out of these gates, we've got a better chance of survival if we work together. If we stay together, we survive. Come together and lock your shields. Stay AS ONE!" The story unfolds as you might imagine. They stay together united as one and defeat everything that is thrown at them.

What if we stayed together "as one"? What if our churches, cities, and nation stayed together "as one"? Would we also have a better chance at survival in the midst of threatening circumstances?

Watching a city unite in the midst of such division is a miracle. I believe now is the perfect time for churches to join together across denominational barriers, racial barriers, pride barriers, and cultural barriers and watch walls come crashing to the ground before our very eyes.

Every night at the end of my concerts, I encourage every person to sing together "as one." We all join hands and lift them high as a symbol of unity for all to see. I then have the entire crowd declare with one voice:

"We are the church
The church with no walls
Shout to this city
Come one, come all
Let division disappear
Everybody's welcome here
We are the church with no walls"

The body of Christ is stronger when we work together, without question. Together, we can take a stand to break down the walls in our lives, churches, schools, cities, and families. Through this tour, we are seeing God set up cornerstones all over the country. It's almost as if He is strategically placing pillars of unity in certain cities and states. Without a doubt, it is God's will to see unity happen in every city, church, and family; but there has to be a willing person or group of people with a heart to see this take place. The real work starts after the event is over. Our prayer is for the declaration to carry on and for people to carry the torch of unity everywhere they go and pass it on to others. (If you are interested in hosting one of these Unite events at your church, and you feel like God is calling your city to be a cornerstone of unity, we would love to partner with you. You can visit www.noahcleveland.com and contact our team there. We pray you'll consider it.)

It's no secret that we live in a day full of division. Every time we engage social media or watch the news, division is the headliner. As I'm writing this, the 2016 presidential election is right around the corner, and every word by both parties is meant to divide. The war on race seems to get worse by the day, ignited by people hoping to precipitate division. Police officers walk around with targets on their backs put there by people who chant division. It's even evident in our churches, as we see buildings being built just a stone's throw away from one another, again, painting a picture of division. We all see these things happen, and many of us just shake our heads. We think to ourselves, How could they do that? or I would never do such a thing. While we may never be the ones leading this dividing charge, we do choose to sit on the bench and watch from the sidelines while it happens right in front of us. It seems we have just accepted it as part of our culture or blamed it on the current state of our country. The numbness and complacency in the body of Christ is sickening. The words Jesus used in Revelation 3:16 tell us we better get in the game: "So, because you are lukewarm, and neither hot nor cold, I will spit you out of my mouth."

A few chapters ago, I shared with you the words used by Mrs. Beneduci from Detroit, Michigan. The rest of the story reveals that Stevie Wonder and Mrs. Beneduci stayed in touch often. In fact, the city leaders of Detroit asked Wonder to do a concert for the city at the beginning of the twenty-first century, and his one stipulation was that Mrs. Beneduci be on the platform with him so they could have a moment to speak to the audience together. When they spoke, they pleaded with the citizens of Detroit to lay aside all racial prejudices and work together as one. The event inspired many to unify.

So what if we could be part of the solution as well? After all, we are followers of Jesus, and He was the symbol of unity. I understand we can't be buddies with everyone we see, join hands with every church we visit, or make a change in every divided area we go into, but we can carry the torch of unity and spread the fire one person at a time. Stevie Wonder fought for unity in the world through his platform, and he was inspired by an elementary school teacher who decided division was not of God. We can lay down the stones we've been throwing and reach out a hand of love. When the Church operates in unity, we see change happen at a very rapid pace. There's never been a better time for God's people to come together, destroy division, and be a Church with no walls!

A WORD FROM THE CHURCH...

By Phillip Presley, Founder and President of SOULSTOCK Festival in Decatur, Alabama

In Chapter 133, verse 1 of Psalms, David says, "How wonderful, how beautiful, when brothers and sisters get along" (The Message). Getting along is becoming a lost attribute of the body of Christ. However, a movement is underway that is changing this. This is a movement Christ prayed for in John 17. You and I are a part of this. By the fact that you are reading a book entitled *Church With No Walls* reveals you want to fulfill Christ's prayer. But a "Church With No Walls" is much more than a song and a book.

Somewhere along the way, we have created a mindset that says if you understand something different than I do, I can't work with you. We will never agree on everything. We have different ideas on worship style, music, understanding of Scripture and even what we can wear—all things we may be passionate about. However, there is one thing we all agree on: the need for Jesus Christ to be our Lord and Savior. Let's focus on this, the most important part (I Corinthians 15:3) and show the world the character of Christ! As we move toward Christ's return, living, working and worshipping together in unity will be paramount. I encourage each of you to take the challenge and begin to actively move toward "becoming one."

TODAY'S CHALLENGE

One of the biggest mistakes an army can make is to divide itself. The tactics for many generals over thousands of years have been to divide and conquer its enemy. Let's put a stop to division in the Church and bring unity back to the army of the Lord, marching forward in victory.

1) **Read John 17:20-23.**

2) **Ask God to reveal in your heart where division may have affected you and your walk with Him.**

3) **Find one person you don't know who is a different skin color than you, and tell them about Jesus.**

4) **Find one person who will join you in taking the torch of unity to more people.**

PRAYER

God, I'm sorry for allowing division to infiltrate my heart. I ask that You use me as a catalyst for unity and help me encourage others to come together in Christ as well. Reveal to me where I have built walls, and help me tear them down. In Jesus' name, amen.

DAY 17:

BREAKING THE BREAD

"And as they were eating, Jesus took bread, and after blessing it broke it, and gave it to them, and said, 'Take; this is my body.'"

Mark 14:22 (ESV)

"

GROWING UP,
I LEARNED
LIFE'S IMPORTANT
LESSONS AT THE
DINNER TABLE.

— CHEF JOHN BESH

DAY 17:

BREAKING
THE BREAD

"I don't like to eat," said nobody ever. Data from the U.S. Department of Agriculture found that in 2011 the average American consumed nearly one ton of food, or 1,996 pounds, of food per year. Pretty crazy! No wonder it's hard to lose weight. #thestruggleisreal We like food because it makes us feel good. Unless you just ate Taco Bell or a chili cheese pup from Krystal, you probably feel really satisfied after eating. When we eat food, it sends signals to our brain, which helps us relax. In many ways we let our guard down when eating a meal. This is especially true when sharing it with great friends and family.

Growing up, my family always sat at the dinner table together. Many of my memories from the house I grew up in were around a farmhouse-style table. My dad sat to my right, my sister directly across from me, and my mom to my left. I remember laughing and telling stories from the day. My parents talked about work; my sister yacked about her teacher or a friend who stirred up drama, and of course, boyfriends; while I talked about school. To this day, I still remember some of the names of the people they mentioned, even though I never even met them. We just did life together, and I was so glad we did.

There are more restaurants in the world today than ever before. The National Restaurant Association projected record food service sales to be over $782 billion dollars by the end of 2016. If you're like me, you tend to scrape up money when someone asks you to go out to eat, even if you don't have it. My wife and I could have just talked about locking down finances for a while to save some money, but the minute we get invited to go out to eat, our money saving conversation seems to slip our minds. We're like, "Yeah, we'll go... Where are ya'll going?" Why do you think this is? I believe it's something we crave. The fellowship we have together while eating builds us up in many ways. There's something special that happens when we break bread with one another, especially when it's with brothers and sisters in Christ.

There is more than one instance where God uses food in the Bible as a way to show His glory. After Moses led the children of Israel out of captivity from Egypt, manna rained down from heaven daily. God provided manna for them for forty years (Exodus 16). Jesus used food, as well, in many of His miracles. He first turned water into wine (John 2:1-11). He fed five thousand (Mark 6:30-44), and then He fed four thousand (Matthew 15:32-39). He predicted the future by telling His disciples about the crucifixion at the Last Supper (Luke 22:7-38). He even eats with them after He rose from the dead (John 21:10-13). The disciples continued this trend by "devoting themselves to the breaking of bread" in Acts 2:42.

Obviously, it was a necessity for anyone to eat in the days of Jesus, just like it is for us today, but the fact that food is mentioned so often in Scripture is intriguing. In his book, *Sweet's Soul Cafe*, Leonard Sweet wrote:

"Food was the language Jesus used to introduce us mortals to the wisdom of God and the ways of creation. Think about it. Every time you turn around in the Scriptures, Jesus is

eating and drinking. These feasts are significant. They tell us of a God of joy and celebration, a God of life and health, a God who offers us soul food, the very bread of heaven."

Many authors in the Bible sure seemed to like sharing stories that took place while eating. To me, the plentiful reference of food is an indication of the importance of breaking bread together and how it can be used for more than just filling our stomachs.

When Jesus broke bread at the Last Supper, He said, "Take and eat, this is my body" (Mark 14:22). Food was the centerpiece at this meeting. The very thing needed for us to stay alive physically is food, which was a parallel to Jesus and His body. What was He saying to the disciples? Most believe He said this so they could share in His upcoming suffering. Eating this meal with Him represented the disciples taking part in what was about to happen. For those twelve it meant they would physically have an investment in the Gospel moving forward, as they were about to be without Jesus on the earth. It also meant to spiritually live meant to "take and eat."

When we break bread together, it shows we are investing in each other. Sharing a meal forces us to be face to face with someone. It also inspires us to let our guard down and allows us to be present with other people in their stories, in their pain, and in their joy. In those times we get to share more than a meal together; we get to share life.

A WORD FROM THE CHURCH...

By Lana Delay, Marketing Director, Chick-fil-A

I grew up with my family sitting around the dinner table. The meal was always blessed, and then my family would talk about our day. Often, we would have a small box of cards on the table for us to pick one and read. A Bible verse would be on one side, and a question was on the other side of the card. It would spark conversations and allowed us to learn a lot from our parents about morals and living the Christian life. My mom is an amazing cook and believed in Acts 2:46: "They broke bread in their homes and ate together with glad and sincere hearts."

I never thought I would work in the fast food industry, but what a blessing! I get to watch families come together to dine and share stories. By serving them food, I get to have a small impact on their lives by just showing kindness with a smile and serving them Chick-fil-A. Not only is the food great, but the heritage is, too. Being kind to all types of people has been my goal as people come to enjoy Chick-fil-A. I hope they can see Christ in me. Occasionally, I have gotten the opportunity to share how Jesus has blessed my life. One of the ways is simply by serving others back in my hometown.

TODAY'S CHALLENGE

Eating together can be a priceless moment. It creates memories you may hold onto for the rest of your life. You never know when it might be the last time you share a meal with that person. You never know what type of relationship might be formed with the person sitting across from you or next to you. Make breaking bread a priority in your life.

1) **Read Acts 2:46-47.**

2) **Ask a friend or friends to join you for a meal.** It might be lunch, break time for coffee and a snack, or dinner.

3) **Put your phone down for the entire meal and focus on the ones you are sharing that moment with.**

4) **Have fun and relax.**

PRAYER

God, I come to You today and ask You to help me recognize the need to share meaningful meals together with my family and friends. I believe You want to do great things in the midst of my meals, and I am open to you doing so. In Jesus' name, amen.

DAY 18:

DISAPPOINTMENT

"And we know that for those who love God all things work together for good."

Romans 8:28 (ESV)

"

THE SIZE OF YOUR SUCCESS IS MEASURED BY THE STRENGTH OF YOUR DESIRE AND HOW YOU HANDLE DISAPPOINTMENT ALONG THE WAY.

— ROBERT KIYOSAKI

DAY 18:

DISAPPOINTMENT

My wife, Ivy, has seen her share of disappointments, so I wanted her to share a little more of her story with you.

When we hear the word *disappointment*, we all probably let our minds wander to one or two major events that have happened in our lives.

Unfortunately, there is no way to avoid disappointment on this side of eternity. It comes in many shapes and sizes. Any time our hopes, desires, or expectations are not fulfilled, we feel disappointed. A major disappointment can stick with us for a long time and even affect the way we react to certain situations. Here are a few Biblical characters, which illustrate this reality, as well.

Sarah, Rebekah, Rachel, Hannah, and Elizabeth

These women were not able to have children, or at least in the timing they thought appropriate. Year after year they had to deal with the pain of not being able to conceive a child. The very thing they were created to do, they could not accomplish.

Jesus' Disciples

The Twelve expected Jesus to be the Messiah and start a revolutionary war that would carry them all to power. Instead, He was crucified and buried along with all their hopes and dreams... at least for three days.

David

When he was only a teenager, he was anointed to be the next king of Israel, only to be so discouraged he often seemed to forget that promise. He was a fugitive on the run while Saul tried to kill him. He pretended to have lost his mind and also tried to run away and hide among Israel's enemies.

Joseph

He was disappointed in God, as well as people. He had a dream, but his life unraveled differently from his dream for many years. He was sold into slavery by his own brothers and put into prison for something he didn't do. He was also forgotten by a prison mate and left there much longer than he thought he ever would be.

Moses

He led a double life, watched his people suffer in slavery, felt betrayed when his people turned against him, and finally was on the outside looking in at the Promised Land.

There are lessons we can learn from each of these people and their respective stories, especially how they all trusted God in the midst of their disappointment; but it's blatantly obvious none of us are exempt from experiencing it on this side of heaven.

One of the biggest disappointments in my life was finding out at the age of twenty-seven that I had Psoriatic Arthritis. This is a disease that attacks the joints and causes intense pain when they become inflamed. One morning I found myself crippled as I lay in bed hearing my son cry. I could not even come to his rescue. My foot was in so much pain, I couldn't walk on it. I literally had to crawl to his crib and pull myself up to console him. After months of dealing with this, I found myself very angry with God. How could a twenty-seven-year-old mother of two find herself battling this disease? I had to face the fact that this disease is not curable and it will only get worse. I was left confused as to why God wasn't healing me. For months and months, I prayed for Him to touch my body but received no answer. I cut things out of my diet that I knew would cause flare-ups, but nothing worked. So here I was at my lowest, so disappointed because the God I knew as Healer seemed to be ignoring me. It felt that when I needed Him to be my healer, He was nowhere to be found. Have you ever felt this way, too?

Although that season seemed to last forever, I can remember God speaking to me and encouraging me one day while I was praying. He revealed to me that I had been so focused on what was not happening, I was blind to the blessings right in front of me. I felt like the children of Israel, whom God delivered from slavery, only to continue complaining about everything they didn't have. I didn't want their same fate of wandering in the desert for forty years, so I knew I had to change my perspective. I had allowed circumstances in my life to steal my joy. I had allowed circumstances to define who I was. I needed to turn my eyes to my Father when I was sinking, instead of looking down at the waves.

Looking to Jesus doesn't always change our current situation, but it does change our outlook. It's difficult to understand why certain things happen, just like this disease that I have to live with, but we can be encouraged that God is on our side.

"But they who wait for the Lord shall renew their strength;
they shall mount up with wings like eagles;
they shall run and not be weary;
 they shall walk and not faint."
(Isaiah 40:31, ESV)

The truth is, the disappointment of only being twenty-seven and having to deal with physical issues people twice my age deal with, is still very much real. The disappointment of sometimes waking up and my fingers not being able to bend so I can play with my children still hurts my heart and my pride. But through it all, God gives me peace that passes all understanding (Philippians 4:6-7) and courage to face it. He says, "My grace is sufficient for you, for my power is made perfect in weakness" (1 Corinthians 12:9, NIV). You and I will face disappointment and obstacles every day, but God doesn't allow us to go through them alone, even when we feel like we're in it by ourselves. We are not always meant to see the circumstance change, but in every situation, we can have the proper perspective. When our perspective changes, we can praise Him in the storm. When we do this, people around us will start to ask questions and wonder where our strength of dealing with disappointment comes from, which ultimately, brings glory to God.

I've seen God's faithfulness in my life too many times for me to sit around and let disappointment hold me down. In fact, I want to share my experience with people because I know there are others going through something similar, and they are counting on me to share my victory. The way I handle my circumstance can be a great inspiration to someone else as they're dealing with their own disappointment.

Let's choose today to change our perspective and turn our disappointment into praise. For me, that means waking up and listening to praise and worship music every morning. I read and quote His Word throughout my day. I even put notes around the house to remind me of God's promises and faithfulness in His Word. I also pray and ask Him to help me have a new outlook for the day. I focus on things I'm thankful for and realize my list of blessings far outweighs my list of disappointments.

TURN YOUR EYES UPON JESUS
Written By: Helen H. Lemmel

O soul, are you weary and troubled?
No light in the darkness you see?
There's light for a look at the Savior
And life more abundant and free

Turn your eyes upon Jesus
Look full in His wonderful face
And the things of earth will grow strangely dim
In the light of His glory and grace

Through death into life everlasting
He passed and we follow Him there
O'er us sin no more hath dominion
For more than conquerors we are

His Word shall not fail you, He promised
Believe Him and all will be well
Then go to a world that is dying
His perfect salvation to tell

A WORD FROM THE CHURCH...

By Dr. Benny Tate, Senior Pastor of Rock Springs Church in Milner, GA

I truly believe that what we consider our disappointment might just be God's divine appointment. Yes, our pain may be God's passageway to a great blessing. Make sure that you turn your test into a testimony and not just the "moanies!" I have found that God used the disappointments and failures in my life to minister to others much more than the accomplishments and successes I've experienced.

TODAY'S CHALLENGE

What disappointment are you facing? Have you given it to your Father in heaven who created you and knows what you need in every aspect of your life? Today, let's focus only on the positive and say nothing negative. Think about all the blessings God has given you.

1) **Read and quote Jeremiah 29:11 throughout the day: "'For I know the plans I have for you,' declares the Lord, 'plans for welfare and not for evil, to give you a future and a hope.'"** (ESV)

2) **Carry your Bible (whether physical or mobile) everywhere you go. "You mean you want me to carry my Bible into a store, my school, and my work place?"** *Yes!* Take it everywhere you go, because throughout your day, the devil will send something your way to remind you of your disappointment, but you will be ready with Scripture to fight it off.

3) **Share with one person what God has taught you through turning your disappointment into praise.**

PRAYER

God, I ask You to help me turn my disappointment into praise. Help me claim and speak Your Word today in every situation. Help me to turn my eyes upon Jesus and look only to Him. In Jesus' name, amen.

DAY 19:

BOLDNESS

"Enable Your servants to speak Your Word with great boldness."

Acts 4:29 (ESV)

"

TO FEEL FEAR
DOESN'T MEAN YOU
ARE A COWARD.
BOLDNESS IS TAK-
ING ACTION IN THE
PRESENCE OF FEAR
— DO IT AFRAID.

— JOYCE MEYER

DAY 19:

BOLDNESS

I've often wondered what it would have been like to be a disciple of Jesus. To walk behind Him in the wake of the dust kicked up from His sandals and see the many miracles He performed. Boy, what a magnificent sight. I'm sure I would have been blown away when listening to how He taught the Scriptures. All those things would have been a great spectacle, but what about watching Him be crucified? What fear the disciples must have felt when government officials came looking for anyone connected to His ministry. That had to have been overwhelming. Even after He was raised from the dead and revealed Himself to them alive, the manhunt continued. He was calling them to go into the entire world to preach the Gospel, but their lives were on the line. Walking into Starbucks to grab some coffee would have been difficult for these guys. Once they were called by Jesus, their life of normalcy as they knew it was over. In that day, if a government official found out they were a follower of Jesus, they would be arrested and forced to pay a hefty price. This would have been a tough task for anyone, as you can imagine, so how did they press on despite the challenges they faced in order to change the world?

The Book of Acts is filled with stories of what life was like for the disciples after Jesus ascended into heaven. One of the most important days ever recorded in the Bible was the day of Pentecost. This is especially true for us as believers today. This was the day when the Holy Spirit came and filled believers. Before this day in history, the Holy Spirit did not live inside of Christians. The same Spirit that raised Jesus from the grave now lived inside of them. We see Peter, who a few days earlier was scared to even say he knew Jesus, now standing up in front of everyone to preach His name. Not only did he share the Gospel, but about three thousand people became disciples that day (Acts 2:41). He received boldness directly from the Holy Spirit that now lived inside of him.

Over and over we read stories of followers of Jesus just like Peter, where boldness dominated fear. Something burned inside of the people of God so strongly, giving them the courage to boldly shout about the risen Savior in the face of imprisonment, abuse, mockery, and even death. The picture we see of devoting your whole life for the sake of Christ was much different in their day than it is in ours. They preached the Gospel on street corners, in markets, synagogues, courts, houses, and even tombs. Nowadays, we have a tough time even saying the blessing in front of someone. When someone asks us to pray out loud, it's like we are given an equation that even Einstein wouldn't recognize. We turn white as a ghost, start stuttering, pass the baton, and then blame it on our "shy personality."

Why don't we have the same boldness the disciples had? I think some of it has to do with what Peter and John said to the Sanhedrin: "For we cannot help speaking about what we have seen and heard" (Acts 4:20, NIV).

I wrote in an earlier chapter that we can't take people somewhere we've never been. We also can't give away what we don't have. For the disciples, it was very black and white. They

> If there is no relationship, there are no experiences to tell people about.

told people what they had experienced. They preached a risen Savior, because they saw Him rise again. They preached about miracles, because they saw them firsthand. Now, of course, we can't go back in time to see all that Jesus did (aside from reading the accounts in the Bible), but we do have the same help He sent them found in the Holy Spirit. The Holy Spirit allows us to have access to the living God. Through Him, we are able to have a real relationship with Jesus just like the disciples had, which allows us to experience God in a real and personal way. If there is no relationship, there are no experiences to tell people about.

When I experience something, it's easy for me to tell you about it. I can tell you the finest details of how it started, what happened during the experience, who was involved, the way it made me feel, and how it ended. I can even tell you the story with the same emotion that I had when it happened. There is a confidence and conviction that goes along with my description. I have boldness because it was my experience, and there's no one that can take that away from me.

I also have a confidence to tell you about my experience when I see you going through the same thing, because I am familiar with it. I know the ins and outs of it, because I walked the path myself in the very same shoes. When I have experienced victory myself, I can boldly tell you my story and how God can do the same for you. When I needed to be rescued and God saved me, He became *my* Savior instead of just *a* savior. When I needed a financial miracle and God provided, He became *my* Provider instead of just *a* provider. When I needed a miracle in my body and God healed me, He became *my* Healer and not just *a* healer. I mentioned this before, but it's worth stating again: When it's personal, it's powerful.

Being bold, however, is something we have to pray about and put into practice. We have to stand up when it's difficult. There's an old country song that says, *"You've got to stand for something, or you'll fall for anything."* I believe God will give us opportunities to take a stand if we ask Him. It's not an easy step for us to take on our own. If it were easy, it would not be bold; it would just be normal. You are not called to be normal. Being bold requires you to step out of your comfort zone and sometimes go against the grain of normality. If you're like me, it forces you to also go against your personality.

God is asking you to be bold. It may require boldness on different levels, and hopefully at this point in your journey, you feel a little more confident sharing your faith with others. So be bold today, and take a stand!

A WORD FROM THE CHURCH...
By Mark Cornelison, Top 5 Finalist on Season 13 of "The Biggest Loser"

My number one desire as my "Biggest Loser" journey began was to step out and, hopefully, let my love for Christ be used to impact others in a way that would let people know God exists and that He loves them. Honestly, I threw myself into it just to get healthier, but God had other plans.

The second week on the show, a fellow contestant and I decided to start "BLurch" (Biggest Loser Church)! In the weeks to follow, most of the contestants showed up. They did not want to miss this time together. Within a couple of weeks, even the production assistants and staff members of the show were attending regularly. About eight weeks in, we actually had a baptism in the pool! Everyone came, shared their thoughts, and left encouraged.

Our church time together was the one time each week we were all able to put the reality TV stuff to the side and just share our hearts and lives with one another. With only five of us left in the competition, we found out that there was about to be a twist we didn't agree with. It was going to affect many people we cared about. So we went to the "higher ups" and asked them to consider changes. After visiting with producers, hosts, and lawyers who weren't willing to budge or resolve the issues, we were given the option to leave. Personally, I came to the decision that I needed to exit the show.

To come all that way and engage with one another on this journey made us feel like we were not just contestants, but family. So, with two weeks left on the show, I faced possibly the most important challenge, one of character and integrity. The right thing to do was to look at what God had accomplished in me through this experience and be willing to surrender the value of material goods and the opinions of others. I left because I believed that those people were worth standing up for.

Many critics have definitely judged me for my decision. To this day, I occasionally still get painful messages via Facebook or an email berating me for my decision. I'll be honest; it still hurts, but that's okay. I never quit; I simply made a BOLD decision to leave. I went on the show to get healthy, and I did just that.

"The Biggest Loser" undoubtedly changed my life. It was used by God to do many amazing things. My book, *UNDRESSED*, has encouraged and motivated thousands of readers. I have connected with thousands of people across the U.S., thanks to various speaking opportunities. SweatCor—a ministry, website, and blog—began as a result of the show and now has over 1,500 subscribers who are encouraged every month. I also continue to live healthier than I ever did before.

After sharing my experience, I want to leave you with this challenging verse and say, I won. I gained the prize that was the most important. Living for God and loving others, that's what matters most.

"Do you not know that those who run in a race all run,
but only one receives the prize?
Run in such a way that you may win."
1 Corinthians 9:24 (NIV)

TODAY'S CHALLENGE

Being a *church with no walls* takes boldness in many areas. Faith is like a team of athletes who keep fighting and fighting, and fighting some more, until one day they know they are a force to be reckoned with and have the confidence they will win every time.

1) **Read Romans 1:16 and Acts 9:20-31.** Note that Saul, who is now Paul, was one of the men who persecuted the early Church. He was even involved in the stoning of Stephen. God comes to Saul on Damascus Road and changes his life. After his conversion, he immediately starts preaching boldly everywhere he goes.

2) **Find a friend, and share an experience that you've had when God became personal to you.** Do you consider Him *your* healer, *your* provider, *your* Savior, or maybe even *your* protector? Whatever experiences you've had that allowed God to become personal to you, share that.

PRAYER

God, I come boldly to You today and ask that You give me confidence and boldness. Please give me the courage to share my personal story. Let the Holy Spirit lead, guide, and strengthen me today as I carry out this bold challenge. In Jesus' name, amen.

DAY 20:
SALVATION

"For everyone who calls on the name of the Lord will be saved."

Romans 10:13 (ESV)

"

THE TWO MOST
IMPORTANT DAYS
IN YOUR LIFE ARE
THE DAY YOU ARE
BORN AND THE DAY
YOU FIND OUT WHY.

— MARK TWAIN

DAY 20:
SALVATION

June 21, 2000, is a special day for me, and one I'll never forget, because it was the day I was born again. God in all His glory and grace saved me that day. It was the summer between my middle and high school years. It was a Wednesday night in Mississippi at a youth camp called Cross Camp. I was there with eleven other teenagers from the youth group I attended in Georgia, along with my youth pastor and his wife. This was actually the first camp I had ever been to, so I didn't know what to expect. The entire camp was a blast though! We had a huge Slip 'N Slide, team-building games and activities, great food, and really awesome worship.

On this particular night, the speaker talked about needing Jesus, and I knew he was talking to me. The invitation was very simple, and there was no magic prayer to go along with it. Instead of inviting us to an altar, he actually told us to go find our youth pastor or leader if we felt this step was for us. Mr. Jon Mclain was my youth pastor and was standing in one of the back hallways. I remember going up to him with my best friend at the time, Kilby Logan (Kilby was killed in a motorcycle accident on my birthday in 2012). We both told him we felt like we needed to be saved. We didn't know all the details, but we knew we needed this Jesus we had heard about for the past hour. Mr. Jon prayed with us.

I didn't hear an audible voice or the angels singing, "Hallelujah," but my heart changed, without a doubt. We went back to our seats as the worship team played softly, and they dismissed us to go to small groups, followed later by free time.

During free time the entire camp hung out in a common area, which had a game room with pool tables, drinks, snacks, and couches where everyone could talk and hang out. On Monday and Tuesday night, that's exactly where I was; but for some reason on Wednesday, I found myself back in my room alone. I was on the top bunk, lying there, praying and thinking. There was a strange feeling inside of me I couldn't put into words. I opened up my Bible, and for the first time, I began to understand it. It was as if the words jumped off the page and grabbed me. I did this for thirty minutes or so but couldn't stand it anymore. I was happy! I had to tell somebody what was going on inside of me. It seemed like there was a fire shut up in my bones trying to get out. Literally! I had a joy, which made me smile bigger than I had ever smiled before. It felt like I had just drunk a high-powered energy drink.

Many of the kids I talked to were super excited and rejoiced with me. Others thought I was crazy and looked at me like I was a two-headed rooster. I went and found Mr. Jon to tell him what was going on, and he was able to help me understand it somewhat. I remember him saying to me, "Noah, you just got saved." I probably didn't sleep a wink that night, but there was no one in the world who could take what had happened away from me.

When I returned home from camp, I sat in my parents' living room telling them all about it. My parents weren't Christians, and I could tell they weren't quite sure what to think about it, but they were happy. I told them things that I needed to change about myself, as following Jesus required me to change some things. Not really knowing much about this salvation thing at the time, I threw away all of my secular CDs and convinced one of my great friends to do the same. I called Mr. Jon and begged him to get me the music that we sang at camp. Passion had just come out with the *Better Is One Day* album, so his wife actually recorded a copy for me on a blank cassette tape (Shhh, please don't tell Louie Giglio). I knew I needed to sing and hear those worship songs again and again. I went to every Christian concert I could find, as well as every church service I could attend. My life had truly been changed, and I knew who had changed it.

The months and even years following that pivotal week in June were really simple. I followed and learned about Jesus and then told everyone I could about Him. I would share Christ with my high school teachers, peers in class, and family at home. I still remember when my English teacher pulled me aside after class one day and told me to "quit preaching to her in my papers."

After a while something changed, though. I began to hang out with friends instead of going to youth group. I would sleep in on Sundays rather than go to church. The "See You at the Pole" group I helped start took a hit when I stopped being consistent on Friday mornings. I wasn't sharing Jesus with people anymore. The fire that burned so deep inside of me had grown dim. I still went to church for special events or when I had opportunities to sing at different churches around town, but other than that, I was a no show. I even started dating my future wife at church. However, even though many saw me as "on fire" for Jesus, God had taken a back seat in my life.

Over the next few years, as I graduated high school and went off to college, I grew much closer to God again without a doubt, but my outward faith pretty much stayed the same. I learned a ton about Scripture in college and even spent a lot of time in prayer with God. The only issue was, for the most part, I kept it all to myself. It was hard for me to share Jesus with anyone unless I was on stage. Despite not being vocal with my faith, my giftings as a singer, musician, and worship leader grew by leaps and bounds. Doors in music and ministry began to fly open. My eyes were blinded during this time because of all the opportunities. I thought because I was in church on a stage telling people about Jesus, I was doing what I was called to do. Even though God was using me to minister to people during this time, I had still missed the boat by a wide margin.

Honestly, it wasn't until a few years ago when God gave me the song "Church With No Walls" that my eyes were really opened. I realized how important it was to tell people about my salvation. This book I am writing to challenge you is basically a set of challenges given to me by God for my own life. I had become complacent. Even though I ministered in front of thousands, I couldn't do the simple task a disciple of Jesus should be doing every day—sharing my salvation story with others. Why had all these things become so difficult for me?

God began to challenge me over and over with simple tasks, many I have addressed in this book. He sent people into my life who modeled this for me so I could see firsthand what being a follower of Christ really looks like outside of a church building. I learned that I have to be the Church in my home, on the golf course, at a restaurant, at the grocery store, at the gas station, and on social media. Over the past few years, I feel I have finally started to get back to being the person I was right after being born again, and I pray that I can continue to fan that flame.

A WORD FROM THE CHURCH...

By David Maguire, Student Pastor at Northridge Church in Thomaston, GA

We are a sent generation! I once heard someone say, "You don't measure a church by its seating capacity; but instead, you measure a church by its sending capacity." The fact is, we have all been sent. God has commissioned us all to GO into all the world and preach the Gospel to every creature. Jesus' last words are recorded in Acts 1:8, right before He left to go to Heaven, and He challenged the disciples to be His witnesses to the ends of the earth. We must live sent...because we are Plan A...and there is no Plan B.

TODAY'S CHALLENGE

Salvation is only the beginning for us as believers. It is the start of a new journey, which will take us many exciting places. It is important that we don't forget the significance of our salvation experience. Sharing it with people can be a valuable tool. It is also imperative that we know how to lead other people to salvation; so investing time to learn and practice this would be wise.

1) **Read Romans 10:9-15.**

2) **Tell someone you know really well, in as much detail as you can remember, about your salvation experience.**

3) **Pray for God to lead you to someone today who doesn't know Him.** When the opportunity is right, share your salvation experience with them. After you are finished, ask them if they want to know Jesus as well. If they say, "Yes," lead them in the prayer below. Have them repeat it after you. But before you say the prayer with them, let them know there are no magic words or a one-size-fits-all prayer that can save them, but rather, their heart sincerely crying out to God for salvation is the key. If they choose to pray with you, follow up with them in the days ahead to see how they are doing. You may even want to invite them to come with you to church.

PRAYER

God, I come to You right now and ask You to forgive me. I know I am a sinner and need You to save me. I believe Jesus is the Son of God. I believe He died for me so I could have eternal life. I believe You raised Him from the dead on the third day, and He is alive today. I ask that You be alive in my heart right now, as well. In Jesus' name, amen.

DAY 21:

PAY IT FORWARD

"Give, and it will be given to you. Good measure, pressed down, shaken together, running over, will be put into your lap. For with the measure you use it will be measured back to you."

Luke 6:38 (ESV)

"

WE CAN'T HELP
EVERYONE,
BUT EVERYONE
CAN HELP
SOMEONE.

— RONALD REAGAN

DAY 21:
PAY IT
FORWARD

Over the past three weeks, you've been challenged to do some really uncomfortable things. Some challenges have been harder than others. Most of them likely went against your natural inclinations and personality and may have encouraged you to step outside your comfort zone. I want to personally thank you for accepting each challenge. I pray you have been forever changed by what you've read and put into practice. I pray your faith has been stretched by it, and that you were inspired to serve others. I hope the challenges and exercises have transformed uncomfortable into easy and more natural. So this leads us to one final question: Where do we go from here?

Let me begin to answer that by telling you a story... One day I was in the drive-thru line at Chick-fil-A with my family, and a really cool thing happened. We pulled up to the window to pay for our food, and the cashier said the car ahead of us had already paid for our meal. We were shocked and immediately wondered who it was. *It had to have been someone we knew,* we thought; but we didn't recognize the car and regardless, we were thankful.

The cashier then told us that for the past few hours, every car had been paying it forward, and people had been paying for the vehicle behind them. So she asked us, "Would you like to continue the trend and pay for the person's food that's in the vehicle behind you?" Without even thinking about it, we said, "Of course!" We didn't even consider the fact that the cost of their food might be way more expensive than ours. The people behind us could have been picking up lunch for their entire workplace, and the total could have been five times the cost of ours, but we weren't worried about that. In that moment, it didn't matter. All we knew was we were inspired to be a part of something bigger than ourselves.

I know the marketing manager of that Chick-fil-A and later asked her about what went on that day. She was blown away by it, as well. She said it continued for seventy-eight straight orders. Wow, can you believe that? Seventy-eight people in a row paid it forward. The love and servant-hood on display that day was incredibly powerful. The craziest thing about the whole situation was that all the people who participated would never get recognized for their gesture. It was a completely selfless act. Usually, when we do something good, our fleshly man wants a little pat on the back. We feel better about ourselves and feel it's imperative for others to know, especially the person in which we served. This model, however, was the complete opposite and something we would be wise to remember.

So what if you could be a part of something like the Chick-fil-A "pay it forward" moment today? Many of the challenges you've been doing have already required you to serve other people. Can you imagine what would happen if the person you served did the same thing for someone else, and then that person continued the trend? We would see an explosion in the body of Christ, all because of what was happening outside the walls of the Church. The Church would start resembling what it looked like in the book of Acts. We would start to see people following Jesus all over the world, and revival would break out.

> The flame is burning strong, and it's now up to you to take it everywhere you go.

I don't know about you, but I would love to be in on that. Good news! We can be.

Every person has a torch, and the challenges presented in this book have equipped you with a fire to carry it. The flame is burning strong, and it's now up to you to take it everywhere you go. I hope it becomes a priority in your life to pass the torch on to the next person.

Passing a torch is a powerful symbol. I still remember as a ten-year-old kid watching one of our hometown hero's carry the Olympic torch through our town square in the 1996 Summer Olympics torch relay. This relay was run from April 27 until July 19 prior to the 1996 Summer Olympics in Atlanta. This run covered almost seventeen thousand miles across the United States. It included a trek on the Pony Express, a ride on the Union Pacific Railroad, and was taken into space for the first time ever. The relay involved over twelve thousand torchbearers, including Muhammad Ali who lit the Olympic cauldron at the opening ceremony. Still to this day, I can remember him lighting that big torch because just a few days earlier, I was a part of it while it was carried through the streets of Thomaston, GA.

Passing the torch and paying it forward may look like giving this book away to someone God leads you to give it to. If you complete the challenges in this book, only to let your flame extinguish when you pass it on to the next person, you would be missing the point entirely. These challenges are meant to instill a *church with no walls* lifestyle and mentality into you. They are meant to, in some ways, help you *unlearn* how you've been doing certain things and strive to do them the way Jesus taught His disciples. Within the pages of this book, you were led on a journey you'll hopefully be on for the rest of your life. This book is an invitation to see your faith work like you've never imagined. Hopefully, along the way, you've experienced an encounter with God, which leaves you inspired, changed, and equipped.

In the introduction to this book, I encouraged you to take notes after each challenge was completed. If you did so, reflect back on the last twenty-one days and see what God did in and through you. If you didn't take any notes, now is a great opportunity to write about your experiences while they are still fresh on your mind.

If you lead a small group, Sunday school class, youth group, ministry, or business; pastor a church; or maintain any type of leadership position, this book is a great tool to help everyone you lead journey together and, hopefully, see revival break out in your circles. No matter what this book looks like for you tomorrow, it's crucial that you continue on the journey that began within these pages.

A WORD FROM THE CHURCH...
By Roger Davis President, YM 360 & Executive Director, Servant Life

There are two words that I often emphasize with our team... Are we making consumers of the Gospel or conduits? There is a big difference in those two concepts. A consumer can become very self-focused. It becomes all about me! How do I feel about what is being provided for me? Am I getting what I want or need?

While a conduit, by definition, is a channel for something else. Think about a pipe that delivers fresh water from an underwater well to people who need it. When you think about who we are called to be as Christ followers, it is just like a conduit. Yes, the Gospel is for you and me, but it is also for everyone on the planet. And one of the things I love about our God is He invites you and me into His plan to reach others by sharing His Good News!

As you wrap up your twenty-one days, I hope you have a renewed sense of the power of the Gospel within you, and I also hope you are ready to take the next step and experience the power of the Gospel through you as you pay it forward to someone else. Go for it! Become a conduit of love through giving, outreach, unity, boldness, and salvation. Be all that God has created you to be. After all, the world is waiting.

"And Jesus came and said to them, 'All authority in heaven and on earth has been given to me. Go therefore and make disciples of all nations, baptizing them in the name of the Father and of the Son and of the Holy Spirit, teaching them to observe all that I have commanded you. And behold, I am with you always, to the end of the age.'"
(Matthew 28:18-20, ESV)

TODAY'S CHALLENGE

The flame is now yours to carry, so carry it with boldness. Everyone has their own torch, so it's time to pass the flame onto someone else and let them start their own journey into the *Church With No Walls 21-Day Challenge!*

1) **Read Luke 6:38.**

2) **Ask God to reveal the person to whom you need to give this book.** When you find the right person, challenge them with boldness and sincerity. Let them know what God has done in your life over the past twenty-one days and how it carries a weight they should take seriously. Let them know God led you to give them the book. Ask them if they are willing to take the challenge. If, for some reason, they say no, then pray God will lead you to the next person.

3) **Ask God to reveal what your future journey should look like based on what** He's taught you through this book.

PRAYER

God, I thank You for the journey I have been on the past twenty-one days. I ask You to help me continue on this road You have led me down, and I ask that I would be a light to others. Reveal to me who I need to pass this challenge book to next, and help me to do it with courage and boldness. Prepare their hearts to receive it. I thank You for blessing me to know that You are using me in Your Kingdom. Let my heart be filled with compassion in the days ahead, and lead me to places and people who need You. In Jesus' name, amen.

I TOOK THE CHALLENGE

Please sign your name before paying it forward!

NAME	DATE

GO.

READINESS

"God called to him...and he said, 'Here I am.'"

(Exodus 3:4, ESV)

"When God speaks, many of us are like men in a fog, we give no answer. Moses' reply revealed that he was somewhere. Readiness means a right relationship to God and a knowledge of where we are at present. We are so busy telling God where we would like to go. The man or woman who is ready for God and His work is the one who carries off the prize when the summons comes. We wait with the idea of some great opportunity, something sensational, and when it comes we are quick to cry, "Here am I." Whenever Jesus Christ is in the ascendant, we are there, but we are not ready for an obscure duty.

Readiness for God means that we are ready to do the tiniest little thing or the great big thing, it makes no difference. We have no choice in what we do, whatever God's program may be, we are there, ready. When any duty presents itself, we hear God's voice as Our Lord heard His Father's voice, and we are ready for it with all the alertness of our love for Him. Jesus Christ expects to do with us as His Father did with Him. He can put us where He likes, in pleasant duties or in mean duties, because the union is that of the Father and Himself. "That they may be one, even as We are one."

Be ready for the sudden surprise visits of God. A ready person never needs to get ready. Think of the time we waste trying to get ready when God has called! The burning bush is a symbol of everything that surrounds the ready soul; it is ablaze with the presence of God."

ABOUT THE AUTHOR
NOAH CLEVELAND

Noah Cleveland and his wife Ivy started Be Loud Ministries in 2008 after hearing a call from God to spread his word through music and preaching. From their home base in McDonough, GA, the Clevelands travel with their two sons ministering across the U.S. Noah has shared stages with For King and Country, Sadie Robertson, David Crowder, Tony Nolan, Building 429, Tenth Avenue North, Big Daddy Weave and a host of others while performing at Christian music festivals and conferences throughout the United States.

noahcleveland.com
#churchwithnowalls

CONNECT WITH NOAH

 @noahclevelandmusic

 @noahcleveland

 @noahcleveland

 Noah Cleveland Music

WWW.**NOAHCLEVELAND**.COM

SPEAKING

Noah would love to speak at your event or host an outreach/friend day at your church. To book Noah to speak please email:
beloudministries@gmail.com

MUSIC

Noah would love to minister at your festival, revival, conference, night of worship, or Sunday Service. He has shared stages with For King and Country, Ssdie Robertson, David Crowder, Tony Nolan, Building 429, Big Daddy Weave, Tenth Avenue North and a host of others all over the United States. To book Noah to lead worship please email:
keith@artistgardenentertainment.com

WWW.**NOAHCLEVELAND**.COM

BREAK DOWN THE WALLS IN YOUR SMALL GROUP.

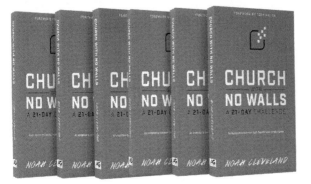

The No Walls Group Package is perfect for your small group, Sunday school class, leadership class, church staff, or family. Take the journey together while keeping one other accountible each time you meet, by discussing the challenges from the book that you faced outisde the walls.

WWW.**NOAHCLEVELAND**.COM

CHURCH WITH
NO WALLS WEEK

Sunday am
Friends & Family Day

Sunday pm
Couple's Night

Monday
Worship Night

Tuesday
Hymns Night

Wednesday
Youth Night

WITH

NOAH AND IVY
CLEVELAND

FOR MORE INFO ABOUT HOSTING A
NO WALLS WEEK AT YOUR CHURCH
PLEASE EMAIL US AT:
beloudministries@gmail.com